The Season of

Pepsi Meyers

A Gift from the
Dallas Shabbat Project

Keeping It Together!

The Season of

Pepsi Meyers

Abie Rotenberg

ISBN-13: 978-0-9948405-1-6

Published by **Audley Street Books**
info@audleystreet.com

Cover Design: Mark Prospero
Edited by: Laura Legge
Typesetting & Layout: Jim Bisakowski / bookdesign.ca

Printed in USA

With gratitude to the Master of the World.
The source of all ideas and life.

"Torah was the blueprint of creation."
Midrash Rabbah Genesis 1:1

With deep appreciation to my wonderful family and
the many friends who urged me onward.

*"Never allow the fear of striking out
keep you from playing the game."*
Babe Ruth

C H A P T E R

1

Before I speak, I'd like to say a few words.

Lawrence Peter (Yogi) Berra

I t all happened because of his incredible vision.

In fact, I don't believe anyone in the entire world had better eyesight. Well, maybe I shouldn't say the entire world, because hawks and eagles can spot a squirrel or rabbit from more than half a mile away. But I'm pretty sure that no other person, no human being anywhere on our planet, had eyes as sharp as his. Who am I talking about? I'm talking about an eighteen-year-old kid from Johnson City—a suburb of Binghamton, New York—named Pepsi Meyers.

If you're wondering how someone ended up with a name like Pepsi, the story goes something like this: Pepsi's parents, Joseph and Emily Meyers, were both fifth-generation Americans of the Jewish persuasion. Not practicing Jews, mind you, as their great-great-grandparents had long before cast off the garb and mindset of their Eastern European traditions. But they admired the courage of the State of Israel and never tried to hide their heritage. Joe was a broad-shouldered man, who stood an imposing six foot two. But underneath the large exterior, lay a soft-spoken and thoughtful soul. For the past twenty years he had been making his living teaching mathematics at Binghamton High School. Emily was a petite woman who perfectly complemented her husband in every way but in appearance. She read voraciously and supplemented Joe's income by working part-time as a pharmacist's assistant at the local Walgreens. They were not rich by any means, but they owned their three-bedroom home outright and loved the slow pace of life rural New York State had to offer.

There was, however, a void in their hearts. The Meyers were childless. They wore themselves out visiting specialists all over the state, to no avail. Emily raised the subject of adoption, but Joe couldn't wrap his head around it, and life just seemed to settle into autopilot until—shortly before their twenty-fourth anniversary—it happened.

At first Emily thought it was something she ate. But when the nausea kept recurring in the mornings, she brought a pregnancy kit home from work and nearly fainted when it turned up positive. Emily managed to catch Joe on his cell phone just before his last class, and in a daze, he bolted for home to the delight of his emancipated students. The expectant parents' joy was slightly tempered when their doctor told them of the complications and conditions a middle-aged woman's pregnancy might bring. Nevertheless, the bedroom next to theirs showcased a fully furnished nursery before Emily finished her first trimester.

The contractions began at four in the morning. Joe was so flustered he forgot to take along the cell phone he had been keeping next to his car keys for months, while Emily remained serene, seeming almost to welcome the pangs of birth. Of course you knew something like this was going to happen, when about three-quarters of a mile from the exit for the hospital on Route 17, their twelve-year-old car's radiator hose cracked. The engine blew out shortly after. Not having a cell phone to call 911, Joe frantically ran out onto the highway waving his hands like a madman to get someone to stop. Thank God the truck driver saw him and was able to screech to a halt before ramming into Jumping-Jack Joe. Oh, I almost forgot to tell you…it was a Pepsi-Cola truck.

It was all there on the front page of the August 28, 2021 edition of the *Binghamton Press & Sun* the next day. How Joe grabbed the driver's cell phone, dropping it three times before fumblingly dialing 911. Meanwhile the driver thought it might be a good idea to check in on the lady in distress, considering her husband seemed like the ultimate klutz. It's a good thing he did, as he showed up just in time to make the most important delivery of his career. By the time the ambulance arrived twelve minutes later, most of the drama was done. The Meyers had a healthy baby boy, and Pepsi outsold Coke two to one in the Greater Binghamton region for more than a week.

<hr />

They first noticed Pepsi's gift when he was around eighteen months old. The little toddler was terrified of insects, and while sitting in his kitchen high-chair Pepsi blurted out in a panic, "Buggy, buggy…no like!"

Joe and Emily looked around and saw nothing. Following the little pudgy finger that was pointing through the kitchen door down the hall, Joe rolled up his newspaper and got up to take a look. He finally noticed a small spider in the corner of the far wall and gave it a whack. Pepsi squealed with delight.

"Buggy bye-bye."

Joe and Emily looked at each other in disbelief! Over the next weeks and months they tested little Pepsi over and over again, and all that did was confirm their suspicions. Somehow their son had been born with what seemed like telescopic eyes. It also became abundantly clear that not only could Pepsi see things from incredible distances, but that whatever his eyes locked on to, he could track with radar-like precision. At the breakfast table,

Joe would toss Cocoa Puffs towards Pepsi's face— even in rapid succession—and the toddler would invariably catch each one of them in his eager little mouth.

Nervously they took him to an eye doctor, who nearly laughed them out of his office.

"I'm sure he has keen eyesight, but I see nothing extraordinary," he told them after looking into Pepsi's big brown eyes with his ophthalmoscope. No doubt he was thinking, *Wasn't having a baby at their age enough of a miracle? Now they want their kid to be bionic!*

"You must be right," Emily said to the doctor, as she and Joe bundled up Pepsi and got out of there as fast as they could.

Now how would being in possession of the most superior eyesight in the world be beneficial to Pepsi? Granted, he'd be able to breeze through school by copying the smartest kid's answers during every exam...but what would be the long-term benefit of doing that? Working for the Secret Service, scanning crowds and rooftops for hidden dangers to our Commander-in-Chief, might be an option, but the pay wouldn't be great and not many parents would want their kids taking a job where they might have to take a bullet for somebody else. Joe and Emily discussed all of the above, but it did not take them long to come to the conclusion, as I'm sure you've suspected all along, that Pepsi's road to success lay in playing baseball. I guess table tennis might have been a viable option as well, but how on earth does one make a living—at least in the U. S. of A.—playing ping pong?

As Pepsi grew, the extent and scope of his gift continued to amaze. The young child possessed remarkable depth perception, and as a three-year-old he was a whiz at catching and hitting a whiffle ball, even though it would zig and zag like a butterfly. Joe could barely do anything with a ball that would trick his son. He would try an exaggerated windup and then fake releasing the ball to Pepsi, but the kid didn't flinch. And when Joe would zip a ball to him without warning, Pepsi would catch it languidly, as if he saw it coming from a mile away!

Just as Pepsi was the center of Joe and Emily's world, so were they in his. In particular the bond between Joe and his son—who not only spent countless hours playing ball with Pepsi, but who to Emily's dismay, spoiled him silly—was more than profound. Pepsi was sharp and precocious, and he excelled at academics. But it was his ball-playing that truly set him apart. Although his early years were idyllic and sheltered, once word got out about his skill set, Pepsi and his folks discovered themselves living in a fish bowl. His Little League and high school exploits were so far off the charts that *Baseball Digest* had published at least a dozen articles about him before he'd turned fifteen. His then-pimply face had even graced the cover of *Sports Illustrated* in a special edition devoted to high school athletes. You see, in all the years and at all the levels Pepsi had played baseball, no one had ever—that's right, ever—seen him strike out swinging. Oh, he'd get called out on strikes from time to time by umpires who were either visually challenged or didn't know the strike zone, but when he swung he just didn't miss.

That's not to say he'd always get a hit. Often he would smash the ball hard right at somebody or fly out to the deepest part of the park. On rare occasions, when his concentration wavered, even he would make poor contact. But no other high school player in the nation had a batting average that was within a hundred points of Pepsi's. He had slightly better than average speed and an accurate throwing arm. But because his perception was so keen—enabling Pepsi to get an early jump on batted balls—he was viewed by scouts as a premier center fielder. He was also by nature intense, and it showed in his game. Despite his superior skills, Pepsi practiced as hard, if not harder, than anyone else on the team. At the same time, there was no mistaking the uninhibited love he had for playing baseball. In fact, now that he had turned eighteen and his body was filling out, it was clear that he would have the athleticism and physique that general managers around the league salivated over. They were so high on him that if not for the kid from Wisconsin, Pepsi would have been the unanimous number-one choice in the upcoming Major League Entry Draft by a mile. Check that...by a hundred miles!

About that kid from Wisconsin. He was a pitcher named Matthew Slade from Madison, and he was two months older than Pepsi. He stood six-foot-five, and the young right-hander's fastball had been clocked as high as 106 mph. He also had a knee-buckling curve. He was the son of former St. Louis Cardinal, three-time Cy Young Award winner, and Hall of Famer, Francis Slade. Sportswriters and baseball pundits were evenly split as to which of the eighteen-year-olds would be selected number one. Spirited discussion filled the airwaves and blogs, as thousands of fans weighed in on the age-old debate regarding the relative merits of a dominating pitcher versus a great everyday player. By the way, although the entire nation followed the goings-on with curious interest, it was on the East Coast of the United States, and in particular Boston and New York, that the matter of Slade vs. Meyers had become an obsession. Why Boston and New York? Because the worst team in the league is the one given the first pick in the draft, and believe it or not, in this, the late summer of 2039, no teams in the league were worse than the absolutely abysmal and utterly pathetic New York Yankees and Boston Red Sox.

———•◆•———

CHAPTER

2

The Future Ain't What It Used To Be.

Lawrence Peter (Yogi) Berra

Let me fill you in on some recent baseball history. Just about everyone knows that until twelve years ago, the Yankees, Red Sox, Dodgers, and a few other major market teams were dominating Major League Baseball. With pockets deep as the Mariana Trench, and without a salary cap, they could and did buy themselves success. The Yankees in particular flourished. In the first half of the twenties they captured two championships, running their franchise total to an incredible thirty World titles. Sure I'll admit that from time to time a small-market team with some exceptional young talent would compete and even succeed in making it to the post-season. But without the resources to do so, these franchises were unable to hold on to their stars, and their place in the sun was unsustainable. So despite luxury taxes and other disincentives, the same eight to ten teams kept vying for playoff spots year after year…while the rest of the league looked on with envy. But the great economic downturn that crippled North America in 2025 changed the landscape. That two-year epidemic of joblessness turned the great American pastime into a luxury most people simply could not afford. Attendance at games dropped by forty percent, and advertising dollars plummeted. Lucrative TV contracts were only being renewed at a fraction of the original rates. The gap between the haves and have-nots was becoming so pronounced that small- and mid-market ownership finally developed the moxie to do something about it. Supported by the new Commissioner of Baseball, Damarcus Pendelton, and spurred on by octogenarian Hank Green, the fiery owner of the Cincinnati Reds, these franchises threatened to form a league of their own and to their surprise, the wealthier teams buckled.

But that was the easy part. Getting the all-powerful Major League Baseball Players Association and its acerbic president Steven Rinaldi to agree to a hard salary cap, which would certainly curtail and maybe even lead to a rollback of players' income, was going to be nigh impossible. Negotiations broke down time and again, leaving the owners no choice but to go on strike and shutter their stadiums. Although Congress sided with the player's union, the Supreme Court backed the owners. In short…it was a circus. When spring training of Year Two was postponed as well, the players, who in the interim were making no money whatsoever, began to wilt. It was then that the baldheaded Rinaldi stood in front of the cameras and proclaimed, "Hair will grow on my head before our members agree to a salary cap!" That rallying cry helped hold his coalition together, but only until mid-August. That was when the owners threatened to shut down baseball for a third season if an agreement was not reached by the end of the month. Thoroughly demoralized, the players unceremoniously fired Rinaldi that morning, and his replacement signed a new ten-year collective bargaining agreement with the League the very same afternoon. The *Chicago Tribune* headline said it best: "BASEBALL'S BACK WITH A CAP AND RINALDI'S STILL A BALDY!"

I won't bore you with the details of how previous contracts and commitments were settled under the new agreement. I will tell you that the deal had an immediate, deleterious effect on teams that had previously relied on the signing of high-priced free agents. The Yankees managed to tread water for the next three years, but after that they became the bottom-feeders of their division. The Red Sox, having had a slightly better minor league farm system, stayed competitive for five years before descending into mediocrity. The summer preceding our little tale was the twelfth consecutive year in which neither of these storied franchises made it to the post-season. Boston was mathematically eliminated from the playoffs on the tenth of August and the Yankees followed suit the next day after losing a double header to Oakland by the shameful aggregate score of 24-3. As they headed into the last game of the season on the last day of September, both teams shared the dismal and profoundly embarrassing record of 49 wins and 112 losses. In essence the last game of the season—ironically a head-to-head match between the two underachievers—would determine which one would secure the first pick in the draft. It also contained one of the most bizarre innings ever played in the history of Major League Baseball. But before I tell you about that, let me get you up to speed on some other developments in the game.

Although baseball and its stars were idle for two years, the owners were not. In addition to crushing the players' union, they also managed to emasculate the ever-annoying Major League Umpires Association, whose contract was up for renewal as well. For decades the men in blue kept demanding higher pay and expanded benefits and the owners were fed up. William Devereaux, one of the principals in the partnership group that owned the San Francisco Giants, was CEO of Optimium Industries. Optimium developed and sold digital imaging devices integrated with high-speed interpretive software. At Devereaux's urging, MLB commissioned the Massachusetts Institute of Technology to modify a 3D imaging platform developed by Optimium and apply it to baseball. The idea was that by embedding microchips in each ball, base, and foul pole, and by installing multiple high-definition cameras, impeccability in play-calling could be achieved. MIT was given twelve months and forty-four million dollars to perfect it. They had it ready in six, and for eleven million under budget!

The day after the players signed the new collective bargaining agreement, the MLUA received a call from Pendelton inviting their representatives to a meeting in Major League Baseball's New York office. They sat slack-jawed as they watched a video of an exhibition game between two AAA clubs at AT&T Park in San Francisco. The game itself was unremarkable, other than the fact that there were no umpires. Balls and strikes were displayed instantly on the Jumbotron and were announced over the public address system. A mere 1.44-second delay preceded all safe/out and fair/foul rulings. Robinson then proceeded to hand out copies of a new contract, announcing, "Gentlemen, if you leave this room without signing this agreement, AUTO-UMP will be the only umpire in Major League baseball stadiums next year." Not surprisingly, a new ten-year collective bargaining agreement was announced to the media that very day. What happened to AUTO-UMP? I'll answer that question a bit further on in the story. But for now, let me tell you about that strange last game of the season between the Yanks and Red Sox at Fenway.

As I mentioned before, it was a toss-up as to who was the better prospect, Meyers or Slade. So, this game was meaningless, other than determining which team would have the dubious distinction of ending the season in the cellar. Melvin Rapp, the newly appointed GM of the Yankees, and Heather Brackman, his counterpart in the Red Sox front office, had said as much. The Yankees sent out to the mound a late September call-up, the unheralded southpaw Gustavo Jimenez. The Red Sox countered with eighteen-game loser, Andy Brock. Neither pitcher made it through the third inning. Balls were smoked all over the yard, and six of them cleared the Monster in left. Entering the top of the ninth, the score was tied 8-8...when an event that took place more than a thousand miles away, profoundly impacted the immediate future of the Bronx Bombers and the Boys from Beantown.

The Yankees heard the news first. Ben Faraday, their chief scout, was attending a high school baseball game ten miles north of Madison. When

Melvin Rapp looked at his vibrating wrist-communicator and saw that the call was from Faraday, he quickly answered it.

"What's up, Ben?" he asked.

"I tell you, Melvin," Faraday exclaimed. "I've never seen anything like it! Slade was cruising along great. He'd only given up one hit, and had struck out seven batters. But facing the first batter in the fifth inning, his right foot slipped on the rubber while snapping off a sharp curveball and he immediately cried out in pain. He then slumped over and grabbed his shoulder. It looks bad, Mel. Real bad."

Rapp thanked Faraday for the update and quickly hung up.

As they were the visiting team, Rapp could not call his dugout, so he frantically rang the Yankee's equipment manager, whom he hoped would be in the clubhouse with his communicator still turned on. Luckily, he picked up, and Rapp asked him to run through the tunnel to fetch Mickey Drake, the Yankee's seventy-two-year-old manager, and put him on.

"Mickey. Listen to me carefully! Slade's gone down in a game up in Wisconsin. It looks like he has sustained a severe shoulder injury and his career might be done. I don't care how you do it, but we've got to lose this game. If we don't, Boston gets Meyers and we're up the creek."

"I got it, boss. Don't worry," Mickey told him.

"But don't make it too obvious," Rapp added. "Ben didn't see any Boston scouts at the game, so they may be in the dark."

Now you may be wondering why Melvin Rapp didn't instruct Mickey Drake to simply pull his team off the field and declare a forfeit. If you are, it's only because you don't know about the rule change implemented by the league in the recent off-season. You see, last year's final game between the Colorado Rockies and the visiting St. Louis Cardinals was not dissimilar to the game taking place in Boston. The Central Division leading Cardinals had entered that last game assured of a playoff spot. The Miami Marlins were in first place in the Eastern Division and they, too, were assured of a playoff berth. Earlier that day, the Marlins lost their season finale and finished the season with a 92-70 record. St. Louis had a record of 91-70 and could tie Miami if they defeated Colorado. It was in their very best interest to do so. For if they beat Colorado, their first-round opponent would be the winner of the Wild Card game—not the dreaded San Francisco Giants, leaders of the Western Division and consensus favorites to win it all. St. Louis jumped out to an early lead against the

Rockies and poured it on as the game progressed. By the end of the eighth, they were leading 9-2. That was when word of the accident came over the wire. Two aces of the Giants' pitching staff had been involved in a terrible car crash on their way to AT&T Park for the Sunday night game in San Francisco. One had suffered two broken legs, and the other was in a coma. The tragedy was announced at the game, and during the seventh inning stretch, everyone at Coors Field stood respectfully for a moment of silence and prayer for the stricken players. Of course while all of that was going on, odds makers in Las Vegas announced that the Miami Marlins, who were virtually assured to be facing the Giants in the National League Division Series, had gone from 2-1 underdogs to 5-3 favorites. But the Cardinals had plans of their own. Realizing that the safer road to playoff success now passed through San Francisco, they simply refused to go to the field in the top of the eighth. The home plate umpire was apoplectic. He kept screaming at the St. Louis manager to get his team out of the dugout, but no one would make eye-contact with him. Then he and his crew watched incredulously as the Cardinals filed out of the dugout and down the stairs into the clubhouse. A minute later an announcement was made over the boos and catcalls of the sparse crowd of Denverites in attendance, that the St. Louis Cardinals had forfeited the game and the Rockies had been declared winners by a score of 9-0. Word of the forfeit spread around the country, and you can imagine the brouhaha that resulted. The commissioner was furious with the Cardinals' organization. Heck, sports fans all over the country were in an uproar. But nothing in the existing rule book precluded St. Louis from doing what they had done, and they went on to beat San Francisco in three straight games. It was a foregone conclusion that a rule change was coming. At the winter meetings, the rules committee announced that such blatant abuse of the forfeit rule for a team's own betterment would henceforth be described as the Cardinal Sin of Baseball, and any team that refused to play, or that in any way proved unwilling to follow the rules of the game, would be banned from the league, for the entire season to follow.

It was further announced by the commissioner's office that any forfeit not the result of on-field injuries, such as unruly behavior by the home team crowd, would lead to an automatic loss and severe penalties against the home team in the form of hefty fines and/or draft pick forfeitures. The rules committee made no mention, nor did they even discuss the scenario, of a team intentionally striving to lose a game…on the playing field. And that of course brings us back to the unfolding drama at Fenway Park.

After speaking with his general manager, Drake rushed back to the dugout as fast as his arthritic knees would take him, only to find that the inning was well underway, and, to his dismay, the Yankees' third baseman Mitch Hanks had managed to lead off the inning with a triple. The only good news was that the count was 1-2 on the next batter, first baseman Dirk Shroeder.

"Time!" yelled Drake.

"Whadya need time for?" barked the umpire.

"I wanna send up a pinch hitter."

"You can't do that!"

"Why not?"

"Because you know as well as I do that back in 2028 the rule was changed. Once a player, pitcher, or batter, is brought into a game, he cannot be substituted for, until the resolution of the ensuing at-bat, barring injury."

"All right, all right. Let me talk to my batter," Drake said.

"You can't do that either!"

"I can talk to a pitcher when I want to. Why can't I talk to a batter when I want to?"

"No direct communication with offensive players. Now get back in the dugout before I toss you, Drake!"

"Then let me talk to my third base coach."

"Only hand signals, you moron. Now sit down or you're gone!"

Drake thought to himself, *How in the world do I signal to my coach that I WANT TO LOSE THE GAME?* At that very moment, out of desperation, Mickey Drake came up with what was very likely the most brilliant managerial move of his long but unremarkable career. He signalled Brad Kenner, his third base coach, to call for a squeeze play. For the uninitiated, I'll try to describe how this works. With a runner on third and less than two outs, there's a simple way for a team to score a run. If the runner takes off for home just as the pitcher releases the ball and the batter bunts the ball on the ground anywhere in fair territory, there's no way the defensive team will have time to throw out the runner at home. But Kenner looked at Drake as if he'd lost his marbles. Dirk Shroeder was absolutely the worst bunter on the team and had not successfully laid down a sacrifice bunt is seven years. Not to mention that he already had two strikes, and even if he fouled it off, he'd be called out. Drake emphatically gave the squeeze sign again and motioned to Kenner, by running his finger across his throat, that Kenner would be a dead man if he didn't comply. So Kenner shrugged his shoulders and gave Shroeder the sign, after which he whispered the strategy in

Mitch Hanks's ear. Boy, did it work like a charm. Shroeder feebly stabbed at a curveball, striking out in the process, while Hanks was tagged out twenty feet from home plate. The Boston crowd roared with delight at the ineptitude of their reviled opponents and rose to their feet at the end of the inning when the next Yankee batter, having already been apprised of his manager's desire to lose, feebly struck out on three pitches.

But Heather Brackman was nobody's fool. Observing the last inning from her luxury box, she sensed something was amiss. Aware that Slade was pitching that day, she put two and two together and called up his father Francis, whom she knew from her days as the assistant GM of the Cardinals.

"How's Matthew doing, Francis?" she asked.

"Gee, Heather, it's so nice of you to call. We don't yet know what it is, but he's in a lot of pain and it doesn't look good. Might even be the rotator cuff."

Heather quickly mumbled her regrets and rang her dugout, instructing her manager just as Rapp had instructed his.

When the first Boston batter struck out on three pitches despite the fact that the Yankee reliever had offered him three tantalizing pitches right down the middle, Drake realized losing the game was going to be a challenge. Calling for time, he shuffled out to the mound to speak to his closer, Jack McBride. By the way, McBride was an enigmatic pitcher. He had great stuff, but his mind tended to wander and he rarely closed out a game without scaring Yankee fans and his own teammates half to death. That is how he earned his moniker, Heart Attack Jack.

After being joined at the mound by Rip Brown, New York's corpulent backstop, Drake said, "Jack, you've got to plunk him! It's the only way we'll be able to get on base."

"Sure thing, coach," McBride replied.

After Drake departed, McBride proceeded to first throw at the batter's legs, then twice at his rear end, but to no avail. You see, the Red Sox batter quite skillfully managed to not only avoid the sphere being hurled at him, but simultaneously swung and missed, striking out in the process. Due up next for the Red Sox was Maxwell Small, their catcher.

Rip Brown called for time and hurried out to the mound.

I should fill you in on the fact that although Rip was not an extraordinary athlete by any means, he happened to have been wonderfully gifted between the ears. Half a dozen teams had offered him coaching positions with their clubs if he chose to retire at the end of the season, and no one doubted that he was destined to become an excellent manager one day.

"Listen, Jack," he told the reliever, spewing sunflower seeds between sentences. "I know how we're gonna get him."

Covering his face with his catcher's mitt, Rip proceeded to whisper instructions into his pitcher's ear. Jack cracked a wry smile and pounded the ball into his glove as Brown headed back to home plate.

McBride went into his windup and released a fastball that was too close for Small to take. By which I mean that Small wasn't certain it would be called a strike, so he had to swing at it—fully intending, of course, to miss it by a mile. But just before he managed to get halfway through his swing, Rip Brown lunged forward with his glove, blocking the bat's trajectory. The bat knocked Brown's glove halfway towards the pitcher's mound, prompting the umpire to yell, "Time! That's catcher interference! The batter is awarded first base."

He then emphatically pointed in that direction, and motioned for Small to go there.

"But I don't want to go to first base!" Small pleaded.

"You got no choice, Maxie. Those are the rules."

"What if I don't go?"

"I'll have to declare a forfeit, and you know what that'll mean for your franchise. You better get down there right now."

With no alternative, the Boston catcher sheepishly dropped his bat and did as he was told.

Jack McBride then proceeded to balk three times. The reluctant base runner had no choice but to advance all the way home, propelling Boston to a walk-off victory and the New York Yankees into position number one in the entry-level draft.

CHAPTER

3

It Ain't Bragging If You Can Do It.

Lawrence Peter (Yogi) Berra

The annual Major League Baseball amateur draft was no longer the poor cousin of the National Football League's collegiate draft. Its first round had become a prime-time televised event, and it was held on the off-night between the second and third games of the World Series. Damarcus Pendelton was on hand to announce the first-round selections, as were Hollywood and sports celebrities who would lend star power to the proceedings. Thirty aspiring ballplayers, along with their immediate families, had gathered in New York. They had been informed by the League well before the broadcast that they had been chosen as first-rounders. However, to make the evening suspenseful, these young players did not know which team had drafted them, or in which position they had been selected. Secrecy was strictly enforced. In fact, league rules stipulated that a team could be compelled to forfeit their draft choice if it were discovered that they had not maintained absolute confidentiality. Since the actual picks were made prior to the media event, the countdown on the air would commence with number thirty, building up momentum and drama towards the last, which were actually the first, five choices.

Although as a high school All American Pepsi had faced cameras and microphones before, the adulation and attention he received on Broadway was excruciating for the teenager. Pepsi could scarcely remember the last time in his life he'd worn a suit and tie. Yet here he was, being asked to answer questions on the air about what he would do with his newfound wealth should he be chosen first. That's right, folks...wealth! You see, an awful lot of money was on the table that evening. Major League Baseball contributed twenty-one million dollars annually to reward the first five selections in the draft. Number five received a one-million-dollar bonus. Fourth place was given two million, and third place, three million. The runner-up's share jumped to five, while number one was awarded the impressive sum of ten million dollars! The television network also kicked in a one-million-dollar cash prize for the top selection and compelled the awardee to appear in a commercial to promote its prime-time programs. So you can imagine the torrent of emotions and thoughts churning in the minds of Pepsi and his parents. This unassuming, modest trio very well knew that their lives were about to change when, with the eyes of the world watching, they were about to be presented with two embarrassingly large, photo-op cardboard cheques, totalling eleven million dollars.

And that's precisely how it played out. After the Red Sox chose second baseman Elequemedo Sanchez of Cuba, the soft chant of "Pepsi, Pepsi, Pepsi" began to swell throughout the auditorium. Slowly it grew in volume and intensity, and Damarcus Pendelton had to shout into the microphone to be heard. "Ladies and gentlemen, with the first pick in the 2039 Major League Baseball Amateur Draft, the New York Yankees select, from the Binghamton High School Patriots... Pepsi Meyers." Sheepishly, Pepsi walked up to the podium, smiled at the world, and donned the pinstripes for the first time.

The ride back home to Johnson City that night was filled with excitement and tears. Joe was at the wheel, alternating every few moments between whoops of joy and uninhibited bouts of weeping. Aunt Sally, Joseph's ebullient sister, got through to her brother's cell from Los Angeles and gushed about how excited she was for all of them. Afterwards, Pepsi thanked his parents for their love and support and begged his Mom to quit her job at the pharmacy.

"Mom, the high school forced Dad to retire two years ago. It's time you took it easy as well. We now have more money than we'll ever need."

Emily stretched her hand towards the backseat to grasp Pepsi's and promised him that she would. Joe flipped on his car's auto-pilot function so that he, too, could turn around to face Pepsi, and grasp his other hand.

"We are so proud of you, son," he managed to stammer, before releasing a further stream of tears.

"I don't know why you're so proud of me," Pepsi admitted. "For some crazy reason I was born different. I really didn't do anything. I didn't do anything at all."

The question remained unanswered, as they drove the last few miles in a silence that was broken only by the occasional sound of Joseph Meyers blowing his nose.

———•◦•———

Although it had none of the hype of the first round, the surprising announcement that occurred at nine o'clock the next morning had as much of an impact on New York baseball as the signing of Pepsi Meyers had the night before. Being in position one, the Yankees owned the first pick in each of the upcoming fifty rounds during which teams would draft young amateur players from all across the nation. The baseball world was shocked when Melvin Rapp declared that the Yankees had selected as their first pick in the second round... Matthew Slade! You must be thinking to yourself, did I miss something? Boston passed on Slade because the MRI he'd undergone at the University Hospital of Madison had been conclusive that he had torn his rotator cuff. Was not the probability of a full recovery less than fifty percent? While gambling away a fifth- or sixth-round pick might have made sense, Rapp was too conservative to risk a precious second-round selection on a whim. But you know what they say: *You make your own breaks*. And that's precisely what Rapp did. Although the Red Sox had their orthopedic specialist confirm the Wisconsin hospital's MRI diagnosis, Melvin Rapp convinced Yankee brass that it was worth investing a few dollars in the opinion of the world's leading shoulder surgeon, Hans Bornhoff of the University of Basel.

"Yah, it is very good that you have consulted with me," Bornhoff told Rapp in a heavy Swiss accent after viewing Slade's MRI. "I think there is a thirty percent chance the young man's rotator remains intact. He may just have severely strained his spinoglenoid ligament, causing his suprascapular nerve to become inflamed, which could explain the pain. If I am correct, the young man does not require surgery! Yah, send him here to me in Basel for two weeks of therapy. I think when we're done with him, he'll once again be able to throw the baseball."

And good fortune certainly seemed to be turning in the Yankees' direction. Rapp was rewarded for his bold move when it turned out that Bornhoff had nailed the diagnosis. Matthew Slade returned from Switzerland at the end of November pain-free, and he was cleared to start soft tossing exercises. The Yankees sent him to their training facility in Tampa, and week after week he gained strength and became more confident. By the end of December, his velocity was creeping back up towards triple digits. Giddily, the Yankees sent him home to Wisconsin with a trainer who was to maintain his workout regimen and prepare him for spring training. You see, although the Yankees had no intention of bringing up Meyers or Slade to the big club for the season—my goodness, they were just babies—having them at spring training would create a buzz and help revitalize flagging ticket sales. The plan was to have them start the season with the Charleston River Dogs, their Minor League affiliate in South Carolina. Boy, how plans can change.

Meyers and Slade absolutely blew away the Yankees with the quality of their play in Florida.

Meyers hit over .500 in eleven spring training games, and Slade struck out over half of the batters he faced. Mickey Drake and his coaches called for a meeting with Melvin Rapp and begged him to ask the owners to reconsider their position.

"Mickey," said Rapp. "We already have five starting pitchers, and Doug Heisler in center field is under contract. What are we gonna do, pay them but not play them?"

"You know as well as I do that Heisler's on the downside of his career, Mel," replied Drake. "This Meyers kid is special, as is Slade. Put them out there, for God's sake. Let's turn this franchise around!"

"Sorry, Mickey, but I've tried. The family's mind is made up and I can't think of anything that would possibly get them to reconsider."

When word got out that the kids would not be making the team, the Yankees' fan base went berserk. Every sports show became a platform for their outrage. Although most veteran sportswriters backed Rapp's contention that the boys were too young for the big leagues, the Yankees' long-suffering fans would have none of it. Season ticket holders demanded their money back, and corporate sponsors threatened to cut off their advertising. The pressure was relentless, and the Yankees blinked. Rapp was told to trade Heisler and a starting pitcher at all costs. The Texas Rangers shrewdly agreed to take on Heisler's contract, but only after the Yankees agreed to pay half of his salary. Detroit, a team sorely in need of pitchers, stole away the Yankees' number four for two unheralded Minor League prospects. But an electrified and happy fan base greeted the announcement on the evening of March 30 that Pepsi Meyers and Matthew Slade would be on the Major League roster for the season opener in Cleveland. Not that anyone believed the Yankees would be any good, but win or lose, at least the season of 2040 was going to be different.

If you think Pepsi was elated about going to The Show, you should've seen Joseph and Emily. They were in ecstasy, and it had little to do with their son going straight to the big leagues. They had reluctantly come to grips with the fact that for the first time, they would have to be separated. Now God bless, they would be able to remain together. You see, Emily's elderly mother, whom everyone in the family called Grams, lived in a retirement facility in Parsippany, New Jersey. She suffered from mid-stage Alzheimer's, and Joe dutifully drove Emily down to visit her every weekend. There was no way they would have been able to move to Charleston. With Pepsi's call-up—once they found a suitable home in the New York area—not only could they be with their son and give him as stable and routine a life as possible, but they would also be a lot closer to Grams for the duration of the baseball season.

Of course Pepsi needed a Major League contract, without which he could not play that night. Being that Joe had power of attorney for his son, Pepsi's agent Jason Stern transmitted the Standard Major League Baseball Rookie Contract to the Meyers' home in Johnson City and arranged for a digital verification of the signing. You see a further consequence of the economic downturn and the new collective bargaining agreement was that rookie contracts were not negotiated. A first-year player who remained on the Major League roster for one hundred games or more was only paid a salary of $500,000. The rule ensured that no rookie could land a lucrative, multi-year contract without first earning his stripes, regardless of potential. He could, however, earn up to another $500,000 if he attained "key player" status with his club. That could be achieved with three hundred plate appearances for a position player, one hundred innings for a starting pitcher, or forty for a relief pitcher. In addition, if an exceptional rookie finished the season leading the league in any of its major statistical categories, he would earn an additional $500,000 for each title he won.

————◦•◦————

After the retinal scan confirmed Joe's identity, he signed the contract on camera and Jason immediately forwarded the file to the Yankees.

"Congratulations to you both," Jason said to Joe and Emily. "You are now the proud parents of a bona fide New York Yankee. Within a few days I'll email you a code for the season's pass to the player's family box at the Stadium. I hope to see you both at the home opener."

"Thank you Jason," they said in unison.

Emily then asked the agent, as a native New Yorker, if there was a particular neighborhood in the city he felt it would be best for them to live. After thinking for a moment, Jason said, "I would suggest you check into Riverdale. It's less than five miles from the Stadium, but it has sort of a country feel to it, with lovely homes and picturesque, tree-lined streets." He also gave Joe and Emily the phone number of a New York real estate agent he was acquainted with, before saying goodbye and ending the transmission.

When Joe left the house an hour later, he was surprised to see a crowd of reporters and a camera crew gathered outside. "Mr. Meyers!" A sportscaster from WIVT yelled, microphone in hand.

"Could we get a comment from you about the game tonight? How does it feel having a son in the big leagues?"

Joe answered politely that he and Emily were very excited, but were also confident that Pepsi would do them and all of Binghamton proud.

"Why haven't you gone to Cleveland to be at Pepsi's first game?" asked a reporter from 1430 AM.

Joe explained that at his age, with no direct flight from Binghamton to Cleveland, all that running around would be too much for him to handle. Besides, he and Emily needed to head off to the big city early the next day to start the process of finding a place to rent, somewhere near Yankee Stadium.

"Will you and Emily be watching the game tonight?" asked a blonde reporter from WBNG, whom he recognized as a former student from Binghamton High.

"You betcha, Mary Anne," Joe replied politely. "We have some friends coming over to watch with us. So if you'll all excuse me, I've got some beer and groceries to pick up for the occasion. Thank you very much."

Later that evening, Emily and Joseph watched the impromptu interview on the six o'clock news, marvelling at the fact that the camera followed Joe as he got into his car, pulled out of the driveway, and drove off down the block to go shopping.

Before I tell you about Pepsi's debut as a Yankee, you need to get up to speed on how AUTO-UMP had been incorporated into Major League Baseball. Although he threatened as much, Damarcus Pendelton never intended to fully eliminate on-field umpiring from the game. This was for two reasons. First of all, he was a traditionalist. How could balls and strikes be announced by a computer? That human component of the game, with the entertainment value of the scowling and bickering it provoked, was sacrosanct in his mind. Second, imagine the chaos if there were to be a systems failure and AUTO-UMP were to malfunction?

A brief outline of the newly implemented rules is as follows:

- NON-REVIEWABLE: Balls and strikes were ONLY to be called by the umpire behind the plate. This included check-swing confirmation with the first and third base umpires at the discretion of the home plate umpire. Being hit by a pitch and other judgement calls, such as balks, interference, and out-of-baseline infractions, remained solely with the men in blue.

- REVIEWABLE: As before, all other calls were to be made by on-field umpires, using both visual hand signals and audible ones, via a wireless lapel microphone linked to AUTO-UMP. They would, however, be reviewed instantaneously by AUTO-UMP. If AUTO-UMP concurred with the umpire's decision on the field, the words CONFIRMED BY AUTO-UMP would immediately flash on the scoreboard. If

AUTO-UMP detected that the umpire had erred, the announcement *OVERRULED* would be broadcast twice over the public address system and would flash on the scoreboard with the correct ruling. In the case of a blocked camera angle, or a scenario the complex software had not accounted for, the system automatically confirmed the umpire's original call. Players were trained that the rulings were considered to be part of the live action. If, for example, the umpire called a player out at second base but was overruled by AUTO-UMP, and in the interim the player overran or wandered off the base, he could be tagged out by the fielder. The reason AUTO-UMP was programmed to announce the words *Overruled* rather than the ruling itself was to minimize the embarrassment to the umpire who had erred. If an umpire hesitated and did not make his ruling within five seconds of the end of the play, AUTO-UMP would announce the ruling twice, and display it on the scoreboard.

I'm sure you have a bagful of questions regarding all kinds of baseball scenarios, but trust me— the system worked flawlessly. Players, coaches, and especially the fans, adored it. Calls were instantaneous and accurate, obviating the need for challenges and time-consuming video reviews. In fact, one of the most frequented video archives on the Major League Baseball website was *Overruled Up Close*. People were fascinated by the amazing accuracy of the eighty-thousand-frames-per-second cameras used by AUTO-UMP, and by how easily the naked eye could be deceived. With the ability to verify calls made on the field, umpires who ended the season with less than a 95% accuracy rating were given their walking papers. To their credit, it should be noted that, as a whole, the accuracy rate of Major League umpires remained slightly above 98%.

———•·•———

Progressive Field in Cleveland was SRO—standing room only. In addition to the Indians being a popular and competitive team, the buzz Pepsi Meyers had generated back East, had motivated close to five thousand Yankee fans from New York to attend the ballgame. There was an unusual degree of excitement and anticipation in the air, much of it having to do with the fact that a mere eighteen-year-old was starting in center field for the highest-profile franchise in the world of sport. There was nervous tension in the Meyers' living room as well. Especially when Broderick Schmidt, the ESPN colour commentator, wondered out loud why in the world the Yankees would jeopardize Pepsi's career by throwing him into the fire at so young an age.

"Just you wait and see," muttered Joe under his breath, as he punched the personalized viewing option on his remote control. He selected seats directly behind the visiting team's dugout on the first base side of the diamond, and immediately a panoramic three-dimensional view of the field appeared on the screen from that vista. As he, Emily and their guests, settled in to watch the game, the Cleveland Indians took the field to the delight of the 45,000 people in attendance.

Here is the Yankees' line-up for that opening game, with some background information on Pepsi's teammates.

1. **Roger Dawson #24 / 24 years old / Second base / Bats left, throws right:**

   Only the sixth Jamaican-born ball player ever to play in the major leagues, the Yankees took a flyer on Roger, who remains a work-in-progress. In possession of blazing sprinter speed, the Yankees plucked the then-seventeen-year-old off the Jamaican Olympic track and field team and sent him to Puerto Rico to learn the game of baseball. Six years later, Roger made it to the big club because of his incredible fielding skills and world-class speed. Unfortunately, he hasn't hit a lick and has only played sparingly. Last year Roger batted a pitiful .188 in just over two hundred at-bats. Something seemed to have clicked with Roger during the exhibition season. He hit .287 and absolutely wreaked havoc on the base paths. His reward was batting leadoff in the opener.

2. **Alberto Quinteria #13 / 26 years old / Shortstop / Bats right, throws right:**
Entering his fourth year in the league, Q—as Alberto is referred to by all—has been a solid, if not spectacular, fielder with average hitting skills. He batted a career-best .252 the past year, but Rapp considers his ceiling to be closer to the .280 to .290 range. He also seems to be developing a bit of pop and is coming off a twelve-home-run season with 64 RBIs.

3. **Mitch Hanks #18 / 32 years old / Third base / Bats right, throws right:**
The best hitter on the Yankees, Hanks batted .296, hit 28 home runs and knocked in 95 runs last year. He also walked a league-leading 134 times. This was primarily because of a weak Yankees line-up, which afforded him little protection.

4. **Ting Tang #46 / 38 years old / Designated hitter / Bats left, throws right:**
Now in the final year of a five-year contract, Tang has been a huge disappointment for the Yankees. A premier power hitter in the Chi-

nese Professional Baseball League, the hulking import never produced in North America the way he did back home. Last year, he only slugged 22 home runs and struck out a colossal 177 times. However, he came to training camp this year more focused and twenty pounds lighter. He also managed to hit five home runs in ten exhibition games.

5.&6. Ulysses Jefferson #37 / 27 years old / Right field / Switch hitter, throws right: Abraham Jefferson #38 / 27 years old / First base / Switch hitter, throws right:

The two Jeffersons are not only brothers, but they are spitting-image identical twins. Ulysses will be entering his third year with the Yankees. Abraham was acquired from the Dodgers in a straight trade for Dirk Shroeder during the recent off season. Once considered to be can't-miss prospects, based on their stellar collegiate careers as teammates at Arizona State, neither brother has lived up to his potential. Rapp's thinking in making the trade was that reuniting Ulysses with Abraham would make the sum greater than each of its parts.

7. Brian Richardson #25 / 22 years old / Left field / Bats left, throws left:

The Yankees' first-round draft choice three years prior, Brian will be making his Major League debut in Cleveland. Coming off a strong AAA year, Richardson had been touted as the great Yankee hope before Meyers and Slade came along.

8. **Pepsi Meyers #52 / 18 years old / Center field / Bats right, throws right:**
Mickey Drake, wanting to put as little stress on Pepsi as possible, placed him in the eight spot.

9. **Rip Brown #30 / 34 years old / Catcher / Bats right, throws right:**
The ten-year veteran is coming off his worst offensive season ever. He only managed to hit .207, and he provided little power. He has absolutely no speed, and he rapped into a league-leading 27 rally-killing double plays. Brown does retain some value for his stellar defensive work, his skill in calling games, and his talent for bringing out the best in young pitchers.

10. **Evan Tanner #26 / 29 years old / Pitcher / Bats right, throws right:**
Tanner was the only effective starter for the Yankees a year ago. He was 10-12 with a 3.96 ERA. The year before, he was the number

two behind southpaw Calvin Moorehouse, until the left-hander went down with an elbow injury that required Tommy John surgery. Although Moorehouse is back and seems to be healthy, Tanner was given the ball for the opener.

That early April night in Cleveland was a cold one for baseball. Thankfully the wind was calm and the bundled-up crowd was buzzing with anticipation. Little did they realize they were going to bear witness to one of the most amazing performances in baseball history.

The first two innings were of little consequence. One Indian managed a bloop single in the bottom of the second, while the Yankees were retired in order—six up, six down. At the top of the third, Brian Richardson led off the inning for the Yankees with a walk. With his heart thumping in his chest, Pepsi heard his name being announced, and he strode to the plate. *It's only baseball. You've been doing this your whole life*, he reminded himself while digging in. *Don't forget to breathe free and easy, just like Dad taught you to do.* He understood intuitively that having walked the previous batter, the Cleveland pitcher would not want to fall behind, so Pepsi should be ready for a fastball. That's precisely what he got. Pepsi easily tracked the ball's release from the pitcher's fingertips, instantly calculating its velocity and trajectory. A burst of adrenaline surged through his bloodstream as he realized the belt-high offering was heading right down the middle. Pepsi did not miss. The unmistakable crack of a baseball striking the sweet spot on the barrel reverberated through the night, and the ball exploded towards the outfield.

"There it goes!" cried the ESPN play-by-play announcer, Sam Weller, as Pepsi took off for first base. The Indians' left fielder never moved. He stood in his tracks, craning his head to watch the ball majestically soar towards the high wall in left center field. Yankees fans in attendance were on their feet roaring as it landed in the bleachers, thirty rows deep, while Yankees fans watching the game all over the country sensed for the first time in over a decade that maybe the Yankees had a chance...to become the Yankees once again.

Now, don't get all worked up about the fact that Pepsi hit a home run in his first Major League at-bat. You might be surprised to learn that 122 players before him had done the very same thing. That observation was immediately made on the air by Broderick Schmidt, who noted that most of them, though a flash of brilliance may have marked the start of their careers, quickly faded to mediocrity or worse. Joseph Meyers grimaced when he heard the commentary.

"That Schmidt is really starting to annoy me," Joe announced, to no one in particular. "You show him, Pepsi. Hit another one next time you're up."

Pepsi did not hit a home run his next at-bat, but he did manage to hit a sharp ground ball between third and short for a single. Abraham Jefferson was on second base a the time, and with two outs, he scored easily. The game was going extremely well for the Yankees. Tanner looked dominant on the mound, and they were up 5-0 heading to the bottom of the fifth. The rookie phenom had already batted in three runs, and had looked comfortable in the field. Melvin Rapp was muttering a little prayer under his breath. "Lord in heaven, I've never believed in miracles. But I'd sure be happy to reconsider that position if this kid turns out to be the real thing."

Pepsi came to bat with two outs in the top of the seventh to face the Indians' third pitcher of the night. He, too, had the notion that he could slip a fastball past the inexperienced rookie. Not a wise choice. With a short, compact stroke, Pepsi lined the heater over the outstretched glove of a leaping third baseman. The left fielder managed to cut the ball off a few yards from the foul line, but Pepsi, running hard from the moment of contact, made it to second for a double without drawing a throw.

"Incredible! Meyers now has three hits in the game," enthused Weller to Broderick Schmidt. Then he added, "Do you realize he's just a triple short of the cycle? I can't imagine that anyone hit for the cycle in their Major League debut." He paused, holding his hand over his ear. "It's just been confirmed by the guys in the truck. No player in the annals of baseball has ever hit for the cycle in his first Major League game!"

The cycle is a rare offensive achievement. It's about as common an occurrence as a no-hitter, which means it only happens on average twice in a season, or once in every 1,250 games. What exactly is the cycle? Simply put, it's when in a single game, a player hits a single, double, triple, and home run in any order. Pepsi was now just a triple short of making history. But the triple is the most uncommon of all hits. This point was not lost on Broderick Schmidt.

"You're right, partner, but what are the odds? If all he was missing was a single or double, then I'd be getting excited, too. But a triple? Besides, if the Yankees don't get a few runners on base, Meyers won't even have an opportunity to bat again."

You really should know that Joseph Meyers was a man who did not consider hurling profanities to be appropriate human conduct. This was a trait he had proudly passed on to his beloved son. But his frustration with Schmidt propelled him to issue forth a word he had heard from his grandfather when he was a boy and had never uttered in his lifetime.

"What a mamzer!" Joe said.

Emily, who had barely spoken since the first pitch of the game, finally had something to say. "Joseph Meyers! I will not countenance that sort of language in this house!"

I know you never doubted for a moment that Pepsi would get one last lick at history. It happened with two outs at the top of the ninth. Tang was on second and Richardson on first. The game itself was well in hand for the Yanks, who were leading 8-1. The only drama left hanging in the cool night air was whether the kid could somehow pull off the impossible and hit a triple in his last plate appearance. Every one of the five thousand Yankee fans and the twenty thousand Cleveland supporters still in the stands at Progressive Field rose from their seats as Pepsi's name was announced as he approached home plate.

"Time! I need time," growled the Indians manager as he strode purposefully towards the mound, all the while muttering obscenities under his breath. He snatched the ball from his beleaguered reliever and motioned to the bullpen. He was taking no chances. Why should his team and in particular his pitching staff have to suffer the humiliation of serving up a cycle to an eighteen-year-old baby-faced rook in the opening game of the year? He had the best closer in the league in Russian-born, California-raised, Konstantin Gregory Borozov, known to everyone in baseball as KGB. Darn if he wasn't going to bring him in to put an end to this madness.

Concluding his warm-up tosses, the six-foot-ten KGB stared at Pepsi for an uncomfortably long period of time before checking in with his catcher for the sign. The first pitch, a wicked slider that broke over the inside corner, Pepsi sent rocketing deep down the left field line. At the last moment it curved a few yards to the left of the foul pole.

"Strike one," barked the home plate umpire.

KGB's glare intensified. His second pitch was a letter-high 101 mph fastball. Pepsi gauged it to be above the strike zone and let it pass. The umpire felt otherwise, and the impact of the ball striking the catcher's mitt was followed by a bellow that sounded vaguely like "Strike two!" Now Pepsi had to protect the plate. The third pitch was a blistering knee-high fastball, this time four or five inches to the outside of the plate. There was no way Pepsi was going to let the umpire's expansive strike zone punch him out. He timed his swing perfectly and, reaching across the plate, managed to get the barrel of the bat on the ball. He sent a line drive over the first baseman's head, gently slicing towards the foul line. Pepsi immediately sprinted out of the box, his eyes tracking the flight of the ball. When it landed, the first base umpire motioned with both hands towards foul territory. The Cleveland right fielder Jeter Jackson (a Brooklyn boy named after Yankee legend Derek Jeter), who possessed the best outfield throwing arm in the Majors, reacted to the call and slowed down. But Pepsi never broke stride. When a moment later the announcement *OVERRULED* resounded throughout the stadium, Pepsi was already on his way to second. The ball rolled into the right field corner. A hush fell over the crowd as Jackson chased it down on the warning track. As Meyers rounded second, Jackson picked it up and fired a strike to cut-off man Enrico Jimenez, who whirled quickly and threw a dart to third. Everyone could see it was going to be close. A cloud of dust enveloped the base as Pepsi, sliding head-first, seemed to arrive at the same moment as the ball.

"Safe!" roared the umpire, dramatically stretching his arms to their full extension. This was followed by what was for Yankee fans the sweetest of all silences. One heartbeat later, *CONFIRMED BY AUTO-UMP* flashed on the screen.

The bedlam that followed was surreal. After time was called, Pepsi's teammates ran onto the field and buried him. The Russian spat several times in rapid succession, glared at Pepsi, and shook his head in disbelief. Then he dropped his glove to the mound and slowly began to applaud. Each one of his teammates followed suit, as the crowd, sensing that they had just witnessed something that went beyond team allegiance, showed their admiration by adopting the Yankee Stadium tradition of calling out a player's full name. Pepsi Meyers! Pepsi Meyers! Pepsi Meyers! Over and over they chanted his name until minutes later, exhausted and hoarse, they sat back down in their seats feeling an unusual sense of contentment. In Johnson City, Emily and Joseph were locked in a tender embrace as friends and even strangers from all over the neighborhood filled their modest home to celebrate, calling out Pepsi's name in perfect unison with the crowd in Cleveland. After the cheering stopped, Joseph was particularly pleased to hear the on-air concession of a contrite Broderick Schmidt.

"Ladies and gentlemen, I've been in sports broadcasting for over thirty years and I must acknowledge that I've never had as much egg on my face as I do tonight. I take it back. This kid is special. I don't know why and it makes no sense...

but look out, baseball. The Pepsi Meyers era has just begun!"

———•—•———

In the hamlet of Purchase, New York, the Vice President and director of marketing at PepsiCo was in his office, talking urgently on the phone with his assistant. "Vince. This kid is the real deal, and for heaven's sake, his name is Pepsi! Get Creative working on it tonight. I want you and your staff to present, with copy and art, at 8:00 tomorrow morning. If we get this right, we can take over New York. And get me the name and number of his agent. We need a comprehensive deal signed with Meyers by the end of the day tomorrow."

———•—•———

CHAPTER

4

If You Don't Know
Where You're Going,
You Might Wind Up
Someplace Else.

Lawrence Peter (Yogi) Berra

At the frenzied media scrum after the game, Melvin Rapp turned down all requests for interviews with Pepsi. He cited the rookie's tender age and his need to focus solely on baseball.

"When will you let us talk to him, Mel?" shouted a reporter from Apple Sports.

"Well, you all know I'm extremely superstitious. So let's just say, as long as Pepsi keeps hitting, even if it's just one hit per game, he's off limits to you guys. When he comes down to earth, I might just let you talk to him a bit."

It was pretty gutsy—or more accurately, pretty stupid—of Rapp to put that much pressure on the kid. But since I'm sure you're curious, I'll give you the heads-up right now. It wasn't until May 15, after opening the season with hits in thirty-five consecutive games, did Pepsi Meyers meet with the press.

New York City was delirious over Pepsi. Print, radio, television, and social media were abuzz. Online, at the office, and in school, everyone was talking about him. Indeed not much else mattered that Wednesday morning to anyone with even the slightest interest in baseball. By 9:00 AM Pepsi

Meyers had been crowned and anointed the savior, redeemer, and messiah of the long-suffering New York Yankees, and their box office was sold out of season's tickets less than one hour later.

Joe and Emily listened to WFAN on their drive down to Riverdale from Johnson City that morning.

"My, oh my," said Emily. "I never expected our son to be the center of so much attention, Joseph."

"I'm not sure I like it either, Em," he replied.

They stopped off in Monticello at a hydrogen station to refuel, and Joe went inside the shop to grab a cup of coffee. Just as he returned to the car, his cell phone rang. It was Jason Stern. He told Joe about a proposal he had just received from the Pepsi Cola Corporation and asked Joe what he thought about it.

"Let me discuss it with Pepsi and I'll get back to you as soon as possible." Joe replied.

After disconnecting, he sat in stunned silence.

"What was that about, dear?" asked Emily.

Haltingly, Joe managed to relay the details to her.

"My, oh my," she said. "My, oh my!"

What happened over the next several weeks was extraordinary. The Yankees played terrific baseball, sweeping the two-game series in Cleveland and taking two out of three from Detroit over the weekend. Matthew Slade won his debut at Tiger

Stadium that Friday night, striking out eleven in seven innings of work. The Kindergarten, as Slade and Meyers were affectionately called by the press, had re-energized the entire team. Tang was hitting again, McBride was focused, Tanner and Moorehouse were going deep into games, and Slade was brilliant, winning three of his first four starts. Rapp's theory about the Jefferson brothers was proving to be valid, and the Yankees' combination of power and speed was winning ball games. In defiance of all the pre-season prognostications, the Yankees had a three-game lead in their division heading into the month of May.

But the greatest revelation was Pepsi. He ended April with an off-the-charts average of .467. He hit for power, racking up seven home runs and driving in twenty-four. He was not just a star—he had become an unprecedented phenomenon. Pepsi's face was everywhere.

Although Joe and Emily were concerned as to how their son would deal with this instant celebrity, they did not attempt to squelch it.

"If your dad or I see that fame is going to your head, young man, this will be the last commercial you ever appear in," Emily said.

She was referring to her son's stunningly effective Pepsi-Cola advertisement, which ran both nationally and internationally and which aired ubiquitously in the tri-state area. The commercial featured a fresh remake of the jingle, *It's the Pepsi Generation*, accompanied by actual footage of Pepsi's opening-night dash around second and his dust-filled slide into third. What followed was a re-enactment of the mob scene at third base, when his teammates had piled on top of him. As they peeled off, the commercial showed a smiling Pepsi Meyers saying, "I sure could use a Pepsi." The camera then cut to Matthew Slade, who pulled a Pepsi-Cola out of a cooler in the dugout and tossed it to his teammate. Catching it, Pepsi popped open the can with a flourish and took a swig. A dance sequence ensued, in which athletic teens holding bottles of Pepsi-Cola took over the streets of Manhattan. Wearing neon-colored T-shirts with Pepsi's image proclaiming either *Pepsi loves NY* or *NY loves Pepsi*, the eye-catching choreography ended with Pepsi Meyers, in a T-shirt with the Pepsi-Cola logo surrounded by the words *I sure could use a Pepsi*, drinking from a can.

Not only did sales of Pepsi-Cola skyrocket in New York, T-shirts and other fashion accessories licensed jointly by Pepsi and MLB, were flying off shelves all over the world. PepsiCo's stock was up 43%, and better yet, Coca-Cola's was down by almost the same percentage. Both Meyers and Slade were also featured in a Gillette commercial, vowing on camera that whenever they started to shave regularly, they'd be sure to use the sleek, disposable Gillette Terminator as their preferred hair-removal device.

Indeed the two young teammates were becoming fast friends. They roomed together on the road and discovered common tastes in music and action movies. They spent many an hour of leisure time locked in video game battles, although Pepsi, with his incredible vision and reflexes, invariably won. Matthew was a magnanimous loser.

"At least you can't pitch to save your life," he'd tell Pepsi. "If you could, I'd totally hate your guts."

When the Yankees went on the road to play the Brewers in Milwaukee, Pepsi flew out with Matthew a day early so he could become acquainted with the Slade family in Wisconsin. Of course, whenever the Yankees were home, Matthew was a frequent guest at the Meyers' home in Riverdale.

The home rented by the Meyers in Riverdale was a fully furnished four-bedroom stone-and-stucco house on Arlington Street, and had a patio and an expansive backyard. It belonged to Samuel and Elise Hoffman, who along with their two children had made Aliyah to Israel the previous August. Not certain that it would be permanent, the Hoffmans chose not to sell their home, only offering it on the market as a rental. The Meyers moved in on a sunny Monday afternoon in April, the day before the home opener at Yankee Stadium. Pepsi got his first glimpse of the house, having just arrived from Detroit. After taking a walk through, he went over to his parents and affectionately hugged them both.

"You have no idea how happy I am that we'll be together. I absolutely love the house. It's perfect!"

The home adjacent to theirs on the north side was vacant. Its owners were retirees who spent most of their time in Florida. Not so the corner house to the south. It was the rambunctious home of Rabbi Daniel Elias, his wife Rachel, and their four children, aged three to nine. That same afternoon, Rachel came by with a fruit basket and her three and five-year-old daughters, Leah and Miriam, each clutching opposite sides of her skirt.

"I'd have brought you a pie, but it's Passover this week," Rachel explained to Emily, after introducing herself and the girls.

"It's so nice of you to stop in and welcome us," Emily enthused. "This is my husband, Joseph, and our son, Pepsi."

Joseph politely extended his hand towards Rachel, but she bounced past him, putting the basket down on the coffee table in the living room. She proclaimed, "I've not been inside this house for a long time, but I remember it being warm and tastefully furnished. I'm sure you'll love it here."

"We already do," Emily said.

Rachel related to the Meyers a bit about Daniel's work as rabbi of The Riverdale Torah Center, which was located a few blocks away on Independence Avenue.

"It really is both a synagogue and a learning center," she explained. "People of all stripes and backgrounds come to study there, and Daniel is forever giving or organizing classes." Turning her attention to Pepsi, she added, "And you must be the young man all of New York is talking about. I know Daniel and the boys are very eager to meet you. I hope it won't be too much of a bother if they come by later."

Pepsi replied, "It's no bother at all. I look forward to meeting them."

"Well, I'm sure you're still busy unpacking," she said, turning to leave, "so I'll let you get back to work. Goodbye for now, and welcome again to Riverdale."

Upon exiting the front door, the Meyers noticed Rachel reach out with her hand to graze the mezuzah on the doorpost to her left and then gently raise her fingertips towards her lips.

———·—·———

Pepsi was out back inspecting the built-in BBQ adjacent to the patio later that evening, when he heard the slamming of a screen door and the sound of running feet. He looked towards the Elias' backyard and saw two yarmulke-clad, baseball glove–wielding boys starting to play catch with a softball.

"Throw me a high one, Avi!" said the younger of the two. It actually sounded more like "Thwow me," as the lad obviously had trouble with his R's. But he had no trouble fielding a ball, as he gracefully settled under the high fly his brother had tossed and caught it squarely in the webbing of his glove.

"Nice, Dovi," Avi commented. "Now throw me back a grounder."

Pepsi put his hands in his pockets and wandered over to them.

"Hi, guys," he said. "I'm your new neighbor. Do you mind if I join in?"

"Okay, sure," said Avi.

"Go easy," added Pepsi. "I'm really not too good at this."

"That's not twue," said Dovi. "You'we Pepsi Meyews. You'we the best playew on the Yankees!"

"I don't know about being the best," Pepsi replied. "But you're right, I do play for the Yankees, and if you'll let me, I can show you a few neat tricks with a ball. Would you like that?"

"Really?" said Avi.

"Wow! That would be gweat!" added little Dovi.

Fifteen minutes later, the sweet sounds of laughter drew Joe and Emily to the backyard. They observed their son with his arms stretched high above his head, holding a young boy who was trying to pull himself up to the same tree branch his older brother was already perched on.

"Just a little highew Pepsi, I'm almost thewe," said Dovi.

"Pepsi," cautioned Emily. "Maybe the boys' parents wouldn't approve of them climbing trees."

"Oh, I'm sure that if any of the boys fall off the branch, the center fielder for the New York Yankees is quite capable of catching them," said a voice from behind them. They turned to see a tall, slim man of about forty with a trimmed beard. He was dressed in a white shirt and black slacks, with white fringes hanging neatly on each side by the pockets.

"You must be Rabbi Elias," said Joe, extending his hand. "Rachel told us about you and your work at the synagogue."

"And you must be Joe and Emily," he replied, as he firmly shook Joe's hand in return and nodded to Emily. Turning to Pepsi, he continued, "I can see that my boys introduced themselves to you already. Boys, don't expect Pepsi Meyers to be able to play with you all the time. He has a very difficult job with the Yankees and when he's home it's important that he be able to relax and have some peace and quiet."

"Don't worry, Abba," said Avi from his perch. "We'll be careful."

Reaching up towards his boys, the Rabbi said, "C'mon guys, you have to come down now. Mommy wants you to babysit Leah while she prepares supper." Once the boys were down, Rabbi Elias said to the Meyers, "It's been nice meeting you. Rachel and I are so delighted to once again have neighbors. And you should also know that everyone in my congregation is so excited about Pepsi and his accomplishments. I'm convinced the same sentiment pervades every Jewish community across the city, and maybe even the country. Pepsi, you've made us all very proud."

"Thank you, Rabbi," was all Pepsi could think to say in return.

Watching the Rabbi walking his boys back to the house, the Meyers could not help but overhear Dovi's question. "Abba, why did you say Pepsi has a hawd job? All he does is play baseball!"

───── ·•·•· ─────

Boy, did he play baseball. Like I mentioned before, he opened the season with hits in thirty-five consecutive games. By doing so, Pepsi broke the American League record of thirty-four, set by George Sisler back in 1925. Even the way the streak came to an end was the talk of the town. It happened in a game against Cleveland, this time while the Indians were visiting Yankee Stadium. Pepsi walked his first two times up, and during his third plate appearance, he hit one that was caught on the warning track in deep left center. The Yanks were trailing 3-2 with two outs in the ninth when Pepsi, who now batted in the third position, came to bat with the bases loaded. Once again KGB was on the mound, and a hit would not only extend the streak, but it would tie or win the game for the Yanks, especially since the speedster Roger Dawson was on second.

Now, I'm sure most of you know that the right field wall in Yankee Stadium is closer to home plate than it is in most other ballparks. As a result, many right fielders choose to play shallow. Their rationale is that if they play deep and a ball is hit over their heads, it will likely leave the park for a home run anyway. Jeter Jackson, right fielder for the Indians, was wont to play as shallow as anyone. Pepsi dug in against the tall right-hander. The crowd roared when he rocketed a 2-2 pitch on a line over the head of Cleveland's second baseman. Knowing that Jackson had a gun of an arm, the crowd stood up to get a better look at what would surely be a close play at home for the potential walk-off winning run. Jackson had a different idea. Being that the ball was hit hard and directly at him on one hop, he fired a laser to first base. Gosh darn if it didn't get there a tick before Pepsi did. "OUT," yelled the umpire, and the deflated fans knew in their hearts that there would be no overruling from AUTO-UMP. An exultant group of Cleveland Indians celebrated their victory on the field as a hunched-over Pepsi Meyers looked on, trying to catch his breath.

The press corps was delighted. Finally their opportunity to grill the young star had arrived, and the media room was packed as Mickey Drake ushered Pepsi in. After guiding him to the seat by the microphone, the questions came fast and furious from all over the room.

"How disappointed are you in the streak coming to an end?"

"I'm disappointed we lost the game."

"Are you not particularly deflated over how the last out was made?"

"I ran as fast as I could. You got to hand it to Jeter Jackson. He made a great, gutsy play."

"Pepsi, you ended April batting .467. Everyone said it couldn't last. Going into tonight's game you were hitting .475! How do you explain your success?"

"I don't know how to explain it. All I can say is that for some reason, I've been blessed with the ability to hit a baseball."

"Last year the Yankees were the laughing stock of the league. Now, the team is in first place, four games ahead of Baltimore. Can you guys keep it up?"

"I think so. Our pitching has been great, especially Matthew's. As long as that holds up, we'll be in the race."

"I hate to burst your bubble, kid, but other than Slade, the Yankees' team ERA is right in the middle of the pack. You guys are in first because an eighteen-year-old named after a sugary soft drink is terrorizing opposing pitchers. You've hit thirteen home runs and knocked in forty-four RBI in thirty-five games. With you in the line-up the Yanks are filet mignon. Without you, they're chopped liver."

"Wow. I think I'm gonna fire Jason Stern and ask you to be my agent!"

The room exploded in laughter and Drake took the opportunity to grab the mike and announce, "Okay guys, that's it for tonight. We've got Slade pitching tomorrow, so let's hope we can put one in the win column. Now get the hell out of here, all of you. The kid needs to get his beauty sleep."

The Season of Pepsi Meyers

Spring turned into summer in a flash. By the end of the first week of July, the Yankees had a robust eight-game lead on the Orioles in the American League East, and the denizens of New York were hoping they would never have to wake up from their baseball reverie. Pepsi Meyers was batting an astounding .469 and leading the league in home runs and RBIs. Matthew Slade was 11-2 and had already accumulated 127 strikeouts. Pepsi led all voting for the All-Star Game and was so popular nationwide that he would have been named the starting center fielder even had he not garnered one single vote in the state of New York. Matthew Slade was chosen to start the game for the American League, and the excitement had inflated the cost of a thirty-second TV ad for the Midsummer Classic into Super Bowl dollars. To tell you the truth, Pepsi's life was so unrelentingly hectic that he secretly wished he hadn't been selected to the All-Star team. With all the time and travel spent with the Yankees on the road, he felt somewhat distanced from his parents. The break would have been a great opportunity to catch up with them.

The Yankees were home that first weekend in July, and they swept the series against the Chicago White Sox. After the Sunday matinee, Pepsi met up with his parents, who had attended the game. It was early evening when they returned to Riverdale.

"Pepsi, I've put a casserole in the microwave for you," Emily said. "It should be ready in a few minutes. Can you take it out and serve yourself?"

"Sure, Mom. But why, are you going out?"

"Yes. Dad and I are running over to the Torah Center for a lecture that is starting soon. Rabbi Elias is giving it."

"That's nice. I hope you enjoy it," Pepsi said.

"Thank you, dear."

In truth, he was more than a bit disappointed. He had an early flight in the morning to Kansas City for the All-Star Game, and on Wednesday he'd be flying directly to Los Angeles to join up with the Yankees for a series against the Angels. Didn't they realize he'd seen so little of them lately? A lecture at the Torah Center? Since when was anything having to do with being Jewish important to them? He heard them leave through the front door just as he turned on the TV in the living room. Clicking through the channels, he paused long enough to watch a nice play made by the Tampa Bay Rays' left fielder on the ESPN highlight reel. The microwave buzzer went off, so Pepsi retrieved the casserole and sat down at the kitchen table. He picked sparingly at his food for a few minutes, then got up and went to the front closet. He put on a navy-colored Yankees hoodie and his old, well-worn Yankees cap, which he placed backwards on his head. He then stepped out of the house into the cool air of that early summer night.

Pepsi had never been to the Torah Center, but he remembered hearing that it was on Independence Avenue. He found it easily. It was an unassuming free-standing building. Parked cars lined both Independence and the side street at the corner of the synagogue. Above the entrance, the words Riverdale Torah Center were emblazoned beneath a lovely image of an open Torah scroll, which contained Hebrew lettering that Pepsi could not read. Hesitatingly, he entered the empty front hallway. He could faintly hear a voice coming through the large double doors facing him. A poster on a bulletin board just to the left advertised the class.

Torah 101
with
Rabbi Daniel Elias
7:30 PM
In the main sanctuary

Bring a Friend!

To his right he saw another sign with the words *Stairway to Ladies' Balcony*. He recalled having once heard that in orthodox synagogues men and women sat separately. But when Pepsi opened the door to the shul, he saw Rabbi Elias speaking from the lectern to what appeared to be a group of about sixty or seventy men and women, who were occupying the pews front and center. With his keen eyesight he immediately picked out his parents. It startled him to see his father wearing one of those awkward-looking silk yarmulkes handed out by the shul, and he was silently grateful that he had put on his baseball cap. As Pepsi walked down the aisle, he could hear a murmur rise up from the participants, who clearly were surprised to see the young celebrity in their midst. When Pepsi slid into the vacant seat next to his dad, he saw that his parents were smiling. Joseph grasped Pepsi's left hand tightly with his right one, and Emily leaned over to gently stroke her son's cheek. Then Rabbi Elias, who had sensibly put his lecture on hold for a moment, resumed his talk, and the entire Meyers family turned their attention towards him.

"As I was saying, the Talmud cites a tradition that there are precisely 613 commandments, or mitzvot, in the Torah. They are divided into two categories: 365 positive commandments and 248 negative ones. Positive means getting up and doing an action, such as giving charity, eating matzah on Passover, or marrying and having children, just to name a few. Negative means not doing an action. Examples would be refraining from killing, stealing, lying, or eating non-kosher food. When one observes Shabbat, or Shabbos as it is referred to in the Ashkenazi dialect, he fulfills both a positive commandment by resting, and a negative one by refraining from work."

"Rabbi," asked a woman in the front row. "Why did you say the number is a tradition? Don't we know the number is 613 by simply counting the mitzvot in the Torah?"

"That's a wonderful question, Julia. But the Torah gives no clear, unequivocal listing of mitzvot with any kind of numerical association. In fact, if you look inside a Torah scroll, you'll see no punctuation whatsoever. No commas, no periods, and no exclamation points. So even when the Torah tells us clearly to do something, exactly how that translates into the number of mitzvot may not be obvious. For example, men are required to wear tefillin or phylacteries every day—one box on the arm, one box on the head, as stated in Deuteronomy. But I ask you, should tefillin be counted as one mitzvah, or as two? Pretty good question, no? Does anyone know the answer?"

Answers were proffered from all over the room, articulating one position or the other.

"Actually," Rabbi Elias responded, "this is a Talmudic dispute, and there has been much Torah discussion on that particular subject. But what I mean to convey is that had the tradition of 613 not been passed down from generation to generation, there might be, to this very day, endless disagreement as to whether the correct number should be 600 or 650 or somewhere in between."

Many people nodded their heads, appearing to have understood Rabbi Elias's answer.

"But I'd like to point out another division in the nature of mitzvot, besides positive and negative. Each mitzvah falls either into the category of *Bein Adam LaMakom*, between man and God, or *Bein Adam L'chavero*, between man and his fellow man. I do not find it surprising that God demands much of us in our relationship with Him. Be loyal to Me, says God, and do not serve other gods or idols. Remember that I am the Creator who rested on the seventh day by honoring Shabbat. Remember that I freed you from bondage by celebrating Passover. These are but a few examples. Some, like the ones I mentioned, may seem logical to us. Others, such as the laws of eating only kosher food, may be beyond our understanding. We accept and obey these mitzvot because if we recognize God as the Creator of all life, we accept that He unquestionably has the right to make demands of us. But listen to this. The Torah is replete with commandments from God, requiring of us to be kind, generous, considerate, and loving to...each other. Some examples are, giving charity, returning lost items, not falsifying measurements, and, loving thy neighbour as thyself. That to me is amazing! It strengthens my love and trust in God, for He wants of me that which I know deep inside is good and true and virtuous. But now, because these laws are mitzvot in the Torah, I must follow this path not merely because I deem it to be righteous, but because it is the will of HaShem—the will of God. And you know what? In dealing with our fellow man, God demands more of us than we ever would on our own. Do you know that there is a prohibition called *lashon ha'ra*, not to speak ill of another? Even if what you are saying is true, spreading negative information is a violation of the Torah. There are exceptions, of course, but the common practice of sitting around the water cooler and inanely gossiping about another's failings or shortcomings is a serious breach of the Torah. What's even more amazing is the fact that if you accidentally overhear such chatter, Jewish law requires you not to believe it. Imagine for a moment if we lived in a society that followed that standard. How much anger, heartache, and suffering could be eliminated from our lives."

"Wait a minute, Rabbi," interjected Pepsi Meyers. No one was more surprised than the young ballplayer himself to hear the sound of his voice speaking out in that setting. "Do you mean to say that I'm not allowed to believe my coach when he tells me to sit on a fastball from Eugene Singer of the Blue Jays because he couldn't throw a curveball for a strike if his life depended on it?"

Once the laughter had died down—and no one laughed harder or longer than Rabbi Elias—the Rabbi composed himself.

> "Great question, Pepsi. And I'm not patronizing you. The laws of *lashon ha'ra* are some of the most complex and misunderstood in the Jewish codes. But to answer your question in a nutshell, yes, you can certainly take instruction from your coach. His job is to guide you, and if what he has to say is for your benefit, it may be relied on. Furthermore, the laws prohibiting the spreading of gossip and slander apply only when the matter is not already public knowledge. Even my wife knows that Singer can't throw a curveball!"

This last bit of information elicited another hearty laugh from the audience, including Pepsi.

"Rabbi," asked a young man from the back. "Of the 613 commandments, which is the most important or greatest mitzvah in the Torah?"

> "There you go again, David. I was going to pose that question tonight, but as usual you beat me to the punch. Does anyone want to try to answer it?"

Suggestions rang out from all over the shul. "How about belief in God?"

"Good answer, but no."

"Shabbat?"

"Nice try…but once again, no."

"That *lokshon ha'ra* thing you were just talking about?"

"Nope."

"Saying Kaddish?"

"Saying Kaddish is not actually a biblical commandment, although prayer in general is. But no, even prayer is not considered to be the most important of the 613 mitzvot."

"Rabbi, please…tell us already!"

"The answer, my dear friends, is precisely what we've been doing here in this room tonight. The greatest of all mitzvot is to study Torah."

As you can imagine, after the lecture Pepsi and his parents found themselves surrounded by people who either wished to welcome them or get an autograph from Pepsi, or both. Many expressed how proud they were of Pepsi's accomplishments, and some said they'd attended games for the first time in years because a member of the tribe was now a Yankee. Rabbi Elias made certain the hero worship did not get out of hand.

"C'mon, folks," he said. "We wouldn't want this to be the last time the Meyers family came to a lecture, would we?" He took Pepsi by the arm and navigated him and his parents towards the front door. "It was great seeing you here tonight," he whispered to Pepsi. "And good luck in Kansas City. We're all rooting for you."

As they were walking home, Pepsi asked his parents, "Was this the first time you've gone to hear Rabbi Elias?"

"No, dear," said Emily. "This was my third class. But your father has been to the Center at least half a dozen times, if not more."

Pepsi looked at his father with bemusement. "Really, Dad? What's going on?"

"I've gotta tell you son," Joe answered. "I'm so proud of your success, and I'm grateful for the financial security it has brought our family. But I'm also thankful, perhaps even more so, that your career has brought us here to New York. Because I now realize that I've lived my whole life without the faintest notion as to what my own religion is all about. Not a clue. I'm completely blown away by the number of people I've observed practicing and studying Judaism."

They arrived at their front door. After they entered the house, Joseph said, "Pepsi, get a few beers from the fridge and bring them out to the backyard. I'd like to finish this discussion with you."

"Okay, Dad. Mom, are you joining us?"

"Yes of course. But I think I'll take a pass on the beer."

Sitting on the patio, Joseph related to Pepsi what he remembered of the Meyers family's history and its connection to the Jewish faith. "My dad, your Grandpa Howard, told me about the family's move from New York City to Binghamton. He was only six years old when his father, my Grandpa Phil, went to sell insurance for a company called Security Mutual. Grandpa Phil joined Temple Concord, and he used to send Granddaddy to their Hebrew School every Sunday. Dad told me how much he resented having his free time taken away while his friends were all running around and having a good time. He said that was why he never sent me or your Aunt Sally to any after-school programs, Jewish or otherwise. I never saw Dad go to temple, except for Grandpa Phil's funeral. He managed to recite the Kaddish with the cantor's help at the gravesite, but it was the first and last time he did so. A couple of kids in my class were Jewish and I even went to a few Bar Mitzvahs. But truth be told, I never even learned how to read the Hebrew alphabet. If I ever spoke to my dad about being Jewish or about religious practice, he'd get agitated. He said Jews who kept those old-fashioned archaic laws were fanatics. Just look how they dressed, he would say. Black hats and long beards and ear locks…like they were still in the Middle Ages."

"But Dad, don't you agree that those people are fanatics?"

"That's the thing, Pepsi. In the past few months I've discovered an entire world of people who practice what my dad called out-of-date, antiquated laws. They are anything but fanatics. They dress just like you and I do. Many are professionals, involved in business, law or medicine. Others are teachers, plumbers, and electricians. You know, middle-class folk, much the same as us. Mostly they are articulate, informed people who just happen to also be passionate about Judaism. They don't lift a finger to work on Shabbat under any circumstances. They go to shul every day to pray and study Torah. They have beautiful families and they spend time together celebrating Shabbat and holidays. And there are so many of them, Pepsi! Riverdale might only have a few thousand, but Rabbi Elias showed us a video of the various communities in New York City and other major cities around the country. It's mind-boggling! Hundreds of thousands of Jews, practicing a living form of Judaism that my Dad thought was dead, or at best dying. I even met one of those bearded Hasidic fellas from Brooklyn with a round black fedora, and I tell you, he's no fanatic either. The guy's name is Yitz Rosenstein and he gives the beginner class at the Center. He's a warm and caring person, with a great sense of humor."

"He gave your father a ride home from the Center the day it rained last week," said Emily. "Then he asked your father if he could come in the house to meet me. He wanted to thank me for encouraging your dad to study, and for having raised such a wonderful son like you, Pepsi. He dresses oddly, but I tell you, like with all people, you shouldn't judge a book by its cover."

"But, Mom, they don't even let the men and women sit together during prayers. Are you telling me you're okay with that?"

"I asked the Rabbi that same question at the first class I attended. He answered me that if you view coming to a house of worship as a serious opportunity to connect with God through prayer and introspection, wouldn't you want to minimize distractions? You remember how Marla used to complain about Jeremy and Dana, don't you?"

Marla Holmes, a devout Episcopalian and Johnson City native, was Emily Meyers' long-time neighbor and best friend. She often bemoaned the fact that her seventeen-year-old son and fifteen-year-old daughter had little interest in focusing on the sermon or prayers, but would exchange winks and glances with members of the opposite sex.

"I remember," Pepsi said.

"The perfume would drive me nuts if everyone sat together, anyway," Joe said.

Pepsi looked quizzically at his parents. "Am I to understand from all this that you guys are considering, at your age, to suddenly become religious?"

Their silence hit him hard. He wondered to himself, *What in the world is happening to my life?*

CHAPTER 5

You Can Observe A Lot By Watching.

Lawrence Peter (Yogi) Berra

Pepsi had been on a twelve-game hitting streak entering the All Star break, but he went on an absolute tear afterwards. For the rest of July he averaged 2.2 hits per game, and his league-leading batting average ballooned to an inconceivable .491. His consecutive-game hit streak reached thirty-four, and some opposing managers chose to walk him intentionally, even with men on base ahead of him. Pepsi also seemed to be developing an edge to his play. The kid-in-the-playground enthusiasm he had displayed during his first few months in the big leagues had all but disappeared. He scowled at opposing pitchers, showed frustration when a hard-hit ball was caught, and for the most part, played the game without the trace of a smile on his face. Mickey Drake and Melvin Rapp were delighted with the new Pepsi Meyers. To them his demeanor indicated a commitment to hard-nosed winning, which they liked to see in a ballplayer. To his good friend Matthew Slade it signaled that something was troubling Pepsi, and he was going to get to the bottom of it.

The Yankees were home against Tampa that Monday afternoon, and Matthew called Emily before the game to get himself invited over to the Meyers' place for dinner. Of course she responded that she and Joe would be delighted if he came by.

"Your mom called and asked me to come over for dinner," Matthew fibbed to Pepsi after the game, in which Slade had struck out ten. The Yankees had won 6-2 and Pepsi had homered, running his hitting streak to thirty-five games.

"That's great, Matt. After we shower, we can grab a cab together."

Half an hour later they were standing on River Avenue, when a driverless Yellow Cab, pulled up to the curb in front of them. Once they were settled in the back seat and on the move, Matthew started probing. "What's going on, Pepsi?"

"Whadya mean?"

"I mean, what's bothering you? You've become so intense on the field lately. It seems like you're playing with a chip on your shoulder or something. You hit one out of the park today and didn't even crack a smile."

"I've got some stuff going on, that's all."

"Girlfriend trouble?"

"You'd think. But nah, it's just some stuff going on at home."

"Stuff going on at home? Listen, Meyers. Back in Madison I've got three sisters, three brothers, and two huge Saint Bernards. Stuff goes on in the Slade household. But the Meyers family abode is like a library. Nothing ever happens in your house!"

"Well, you'd be surprised. My dad is sixty-eight, my mom sixty-three. And suddenly at this stage in their lives, they've decided to get involved in religion."

"Religion? Aren't you guys Jewish already?"

"Yeah, we're Jewish. But now they're becoming religious Jewish. Over the past few months they've been more interested in that stuff, than in following baseball. Not that I'm being totally ignored, but they've got other priorities now. Just last week they had a couple of young rabbis come over to the house to make the kitchen kosher. They poured boiling water everywhere and used a blowtorch on the oven, burners, and barbecue out back. Mom threw out all the old dishes and bought two new sets, one for milk and one for meat. I'm going nuts, Matt. If I want a cheeseburger, I've got to go out to McDonalds!" Matthew started laughing so much he had a hard time blurting out, "I'll bet you'll be playing center field soon wearing one of those cute little beanies on your head."

"Now you see why I'm so upset. My best friend's already making me feel like a fool. Imagine what'll happen when the whole world finds out."

When they arrived at the house they found Emily sitting in the kitchen with the rabbi's wife, Rachel Elias. There was a large book on the dinette table entitled The Kosher Experience: Rules and Recipes. The boys each gave Emily a peck on her cheek. Matthew had met Rachel months earlier and knew she was an avid Yankees fan. Turning to Rachel, Pepsi and Matthew said in unison, "Hello, Mrs. Elias."

"Hi, boys," she replied. "Great game today."

"Dad's out back preparing hamburgers on the barbecue," Emily said. "We're eating outside on the patio. Matthew, could you take the salad bowl that's on the counter? And Pepsi, grab some sodas from the fridge. Everything else is already outside."

The boys did as they were told, and they found Joe out back tending the barbecue. He was wearing a Yankees cap and an apron with three large chevrons in the center, surrounded by the words *Don't mess with the Grill Sergeant.* On the chair next to the barbecue was an empty carton with the words *Berger's Burgers* and in smaller letters beneath the logo, *Deluxe Glatt Kosher.*

"Hey, Mr. M, it's good to see you. Those burgers sure look good."

"Nice job at the park today," Joe replied, giving one of the burgers a flip. "Matt, I love the way you're using your slider lately."

"Thanks. By the way, that relaxation technique you trained Pepsi with for all those years is amazing. It took Pepsi a while to knock it into my thick skull, but I've started using it, especially with men on base. It really works."

"That's great, Matt, but remember that it goes no further. I don't want every guy in the league knowing my tricks." Joe turned to his son and said, "Pepsi, that was a nice adjustment you made on the change-up, hitting it out to the opposite field."

"Thanks, Dad. But you know, I don't know how much longer I'll be able to keep up the hitting streak. I've been walked too many times lately."

"That's not necessarily a bad thing, son," Joe replied.

"What do you mean, walking or not keeping up the streak?"

"I'm talking about the streak. I've been thinking about it a lot lately. If you end up hitting over .400 and become the first player since Ted Williams to do that, Yankees fans will adore you for taking the record away from a member of the Red Sox. But breaking Joe DiMaggio's fifty-six-game hitting streak might not be so popular."

"Why would New York fans be unhappy if another Yankee broke the record?" Matt asked.

"I wish I didn't have to say this, Matt, but the reason is because….Pepsi is Jewish."

Although most eighteen year olds I know would have no interest in the subject, as the four of them sat down to eat, the discussion about prejudice and bigotry in the world of sport continued. Joe told them about the threats and incessant verbal abuse Jackie Robinson experienced as the first African-American in Major League Baseball. He told them about Hank Aaron's pursuit of Babe Ruth's career home run record, and the death threats he received as he closed in on it. He told them about Hank Greenberg, the first great Jewish baseball player back in the 1950s. He suffered continuous anti-Semitic taunting and was pilloried by Detroit Tigers fans for refusing to play on Yom Kippur, the most solemn day in the Jewish calendar. Joseph argued that Pepsi would be no different. As popular as he was and as appreciative as many fans were that he had brought the Yankees back to life, there would always be a segment of the fan base that would not be able to embrace him because of his faith.

"I don't get it, Mr. Meyers. So he's Jewish. He's *awesome*."

"God bless you, Matt," Joe answered. "I know that your parents raised you to be tolerant of others. But unfortunately, too many people in the world don't think that way."

Emily joined the conversation. "This has been a way of life for the Jewish people for thousands of years, Matt. The Holocaust was only the culmination of centuries of hate. The more successful Pepsi becomes, the more likely it is that anti-Semitism and enmity towards him will grow."

Pepsi threw his half-eaten hamburger down on his plate. "This stinks! I come home to relax and have a good time with my friend and all we end up talking about is this depressing Jewish stuff."

"I don't disagree with you that anti-Semitism is depressing," Joe conceded. "But it exists, Pepsi. Ignoring it won't make it go away."

"But it seems like Judaism is all you and Mom ever talk about now. I've heard more about it these past few weeks than in my entire life a hundred times over. I never once heard anyone say the word Torah until we moved here. Now I hear it all the time and I can't handle it."

"What your mother and I have done has been excruciatingly difficult for us as well, Pepsi," Joe said. "It's not easy making lifestyle changes at any age, let alone ours. You think we won't miss the freedom of being able to do just about anything we want? I'm surprised you're only thinking about yourself."

"Joseph!" Emily said, staring at her husband disapprovingly.

"Yeah, well that's exactly how I feel about what you're doing," Pepsi mumbled, half under his breath.

"Pepsi," Emily said softly. "Your dad and I realize it's been hard on you. But we've not asked you, nor do we expect you, to follow our lead. You are an adult and we have no right to impose anything on you. We will always love you with all our hearts, unconditionally. He may have butchered it, but I think what your dad meant to say was that if you love us as well, you should be happy for us and the peace and meaning we are now finding in our lives."

A tear had rolled down Joseph's cheek as he listened to Emily. He looked at her tenderly and silently mouthed the words "Thank you." He then stood up and motioned with his outstretched arms for his son to come to him.

"Aw, what the heck," Pepsi said, as he stood up and went to his dad to receive one of Joe Meyers's legendary, rib-cracking hugs.

After Matthew had left and Emily had gone to bed, Joe dropped a bombshell on his son. "I didn't want to say this while Matt was here, but I received a phone call this afternoon from Melvin Rapp."

"What did he want?"

"He talked to me about your hitting streak. He was wondering, just as I was, if a Jewish kid breaking the record would be a good thing. He spoke about the pride the Italian community had in their hero Joe DiMaggio, and possible repercussions if you were to succeed."

"So he told you I should intentionally let myself get out, to put an end to the streak?"

"Without saying as much, yes. But he did mention that he'd love to see you break Pete Rose's record of forty-four games and take over second place."

"Did the owners ask him to make the call?"

"No. He clearly said he was doing it on his own, as a concerned Jew."

"What did you tell him?"

"I said I would mention his concerns, but that ultimately, it was up to you."

Pepsi stared into the distance for a few moments before saying, "I've been lucky, Dad. In all my years playing baseball, I've only had a few run-ins with kids who teased or cursed me for being Jewish. Maybe it's because most of the kids I played with never even knew I was. But regardless, I don't think it's my job to worry about these things. I'm a ballplayer. I'm gonna keep on playing the way my dad taught me to play…with everything I've got. Sorry, Joe DiMaggio, but ready or not, here I come."

DiMaggio needn't have worried. Pepsi Meyers's streak came to an abrupt end the very next night against Tampa. In his first at-bat, bad luck robbed him of a double. The scorching grounder he hit down the third base line ricocheted off the bag right to the third baseman, who threw him out easily. In his second at-bat against Hector Machado, the Rays' hard-throwing ace, Pepsi thought the right-hander was taking too long, so he took his right hand off the bat to signal to the umpire that he wanted time. The umpire responded, perhaps a bit too slowly, and raised both of his hands to signal for time. But Machado, who possessed a short and compact delivery, was beyond the point of no return. Pepsi had turned to look at the umpire upon hearing the call and was unaware that Machado had released the ball. Perhaps it was because of the umpire's movement, but Machado's follow-through was awkward and the ball flew straight towards Pepsi's head! I can tell you for a fact folks, that at 90 miles per hour it takes less than half a second for a ball to reach home plate. Pepsi didn't have a chance. By the time he turned back to the pitcher, the ball was a mere twenty feet away. In that tenth of a second he managed to tilt his head slightly away from the ball, but it nevertheless struck him flush on the helmet just above the temple. Pepsi's world went black. The bat slipped from his hand and he collapsed to the ground, unconscious. A hush fell over the crowd as the Yankees' trainer and Mickey Drake rushed from the dugout towards the fallen star.

"How is he?" probed Drake.

"At least he's breathing," said the trainer. "Otherwise, he's out like a light."

"Can't you do something?"

"We don't use smelling salts anymore, Mickey. Give him a minute. I think he'll come around on his own."

Machado appeared to be extremely distressed, and was pacing on and off the pitching mound with his hands on his head. The other Rays infielders walked over to console him. On the grass between home and first, Pepsi's teammates had gathered in a circle. Each one was crouched on one knee and they were holding hands with their heads lowered. Abraham Jefferson was passionately leading them in a prayer for their fallen comrade.

"Lord Jesus our Savior, we implore you to protect and defend our beloved brother Pepsi from danger, distress, and the evil designs of Satan. May you, in your merciful kindness, deliver him from harm and speedily restore him back to full health and vitality."

Suddenly the prone ballplayer's lips started moving and he was overheard faintly uttering, "Would someone please remind that numbskull Jefferson that I'm Jewish?"

Pepsi was carried off the field and rushed by ambulance to nearby Lincoln Hospital. No information was divulged to the media that night, other than that the young outfielder was resting comfortably in stable condition.

The following morning, the Yankees held a 9:00 AM press conference packed with local, national, and even international media representatives. Melvin Rapp was at the microphone. "Pepsi Meyers underwent an MRI last night, and we are pleased to report that the diagnosis was that he only suffered a mild Grade 1 concussion. He has already been released from the hospital and is resting comfortably at home."

"Mel, will he be able to play tonight?"

"No. Even though he passed his on-site concussion assessment, he did lose consciousness momentarily. Major League Baseball rules stipulate that under those circumstances, a player needs to sit out a minimum of three games. The neurosurgeon at Lincoln is also recommending a seventy-two-hour observation window. That's why the Yankees opted not to place him on the seven day disabled list for concussions. If he is symptom-free, without nausea or dizziness, he could play as early as Saturday against Baltimore."

"Does he have any recollection of the incident?"

"Yes, he does. With Grade I concussions that is often the case."

"It's amazing that his injury is so moderate. How is it possible that a 90 mile per hour fastball didn't inflict more damage?"

"After viewing the video again, we think because Pepsi managed to slightly angle his head backwards, the impact was softened substantially. He's a fortunate young man. Both he and the Yankees dodged a bullet last night."

"Did Pepsi say if his life flashed before him in the split second before impact?"

"On the contrary. He told me the only thing flashing before him was the word Rawlings stamped on the baseball."

"Is he upset that his hitting streak has come to an end?"

"He told me he's eager to start another one. Hopefully it will happen as early as Saturday. Okay, that's it for now. My office will keep you updated if there's any change in his condition. Have a nice day, fellas."

Pepsi was rather looking forward to his three-day break. Other than some discomfort from the golf ball–sized bump protruding from the side of his head, Pepsi felt fine. He spent some quality time with his parents on Wednesday and then accompanied them on Thursday to visit Grams in Parsippany. Joe suggested that on the way back they stop off in the city for an early dinner so they could get home in time to watch the Yankees play that evening. Emily called Rachel Elias, who recommended a nice kosher restaurant on 48th Street. When the maître d' saw that the reservation under the name Meyers was for none other than New York's favorite son and his parents, he quickly ushered the three of them upstairs to a small private dining room. But it was too late. Several patrons had observed them, and the social media expressway was soon bumper to bumper with the news that Pepsi Meyers had been spotted in a kosher establishment. Indeed a small blurb and photo made it into the sports section of one of the local newspapers the next morning, under the title "Pepsi Dines at Midtown Kosher Eatery:"

> Pepsi Meyers sightings in and around New York City are rare to say the least. He clearly prefers staying out of the spotlight on off days and free evenings. Yesterday was a rare exception, when

the injured star and his parents were observed entering Carmela's, a strictly kosher steakhouse in Midtown Manhattan. The question people are asking is, could it be that the young Jewish center fielder has decided to become kosher observant? This reporter spoke with Carmela Sasson, the proprietor of Carmela's, who could shed no light on the matter. She did say, however, that after word got out that Pepsi had dined there, the phones would not stop ringing. She is fully booked for both lunch and dinner through Wednesday of next week.

The Meyers returned home that evening just in time for the first pitch. Calvin Moorehouse, the Yankees' southpaw, was starting for the home team. With more than half the season completed, it was apparent that Calvin's surgically repaired throwing arm had fully mended. His record was 9-5, and his ERA was a respectable 3.86. In this game, though, he was struggling. On the first play, Baltimore's leadoff hitter blooped a Texas League single that landed a foot or so before the outstretched glove of the hard-charging center fielder.

"I think you would have caught that one, Pepsi," said Joe.

"I might have. Ulysses took a short step backwards first instead of coming in right away."

Ulysses Jefferson had moved from right field to center to fill in for Pepsi. The Yankees' utility outfielder/pinch hitter Max Durning had taken Jefferson's spot in right. The next Baltimore batter hit a high fly ball into the right-fielder corner. Durning seemed to be overly concerned about running into the wall, and misplayed the ball off his glove for a triple.

"Oh man! Ulysses would have caught that one easily," Pepsi moaned.

Moorehouse was clearly unnerved by the poor fielding behind him. He proceeded to walk the next two batters and then gave up a grand slam to the number-five hitter in the Orioles' line-up.

"Sheesh!" exclaimed Pepsi. "We're down 5-0 with nobody out. My head hurts, and it has nothing to do with getting beaned the other day."

Just then the front doorbell chimed, and Pepsi went to answer it. It was their neighbor. "Hello, Rabbi Elias," Pepsi said. "How are you?"

"I'm fine, Pepsi. How's the noggin?"

"It's not too bad, and I'm certainly enjoying my leave of absence from work. But for the moment it seems like the Yankees are hopeless without me."

"Really? What's the score?"

"Come on in and join us. You can see for yourself."

Pepsi ushered Rabbi Elias into the living room. Joe's face lit up when he saw his mentor, and he rose from the couch with outstretched arms.

"Emily, please tell your husband to go easy on me," the rabbi implored. "My ribs are still sore from his last hug."

"Joseph, you heard the rabbi."

"Don't worry, Em. He's still my favorite. In fact he's my only rabbi."

After a brief and gentle embrace, Joseph motioned towards the couch, and both he and Rabbi Elias sat down. The announcer on the TV had just raised his voice, and everyone looked towards the screen.

"There it goes! Another prodigious home run off Moorehouse, making the score 7-0 in favor of Baltimore." A dour-looking Mickey Drake could be seen lumbering towards the mound to pull Moorehouse.

"You can't win them all," Pepsi offered. "Even if we lose, we'll still be up on Baltimore by ten games."

"They're still a dangerous team, Pepsi," Joe said. "They won the division last year because of Barden and Hathaway, and those guys are not going away."

Joe was referring to switch-hitting Lance Barden, the premier power hitter in all of Major League

Baseball, and Darien Hathaway, the Orioles' virtually untouchable closer.

Rabbi Elias stood up and announced, "I wish I could stay longer, but I just came by to see if I could invite you all to come and join us tomorrow night for the Shabbos meal. Pepsi, your parents were our guests a few weeks ago while you were out of town. With you being injured, this might be the only chance for us to have you over on a Friday night. I know Rachel and the kids would really love it if you came."

Turning to his parents, Pepsi said, "Mom, Dad, what do you think?"

"We enjoyed it very much, Pepsi. Rachel's an amazing cook," his mother said.

"If you're gonna have Grolsch like last time, you can count me in," said Joe.

"Don't worry, Joseph, I've already picked up a keg."

"Well, I don't want to be the only one missing out," Pepsi said. "Thank you, Rabbi. You can count me in."

———•◦•———

Joseph Meyers had been attending shul on Shabbos for several weeks now, and he loved it. Late in the day on Friday, he asked his son if he'd like to come along, but Pepsi demurred. Joseph did not press him, and he left home just before 7:00 PM. An hour later, Emily told Pepsi that they should head next door so they could be at the Elias's home when Joe and Daniel returned from the prayer services. Approaching their neighbor's front door, Pepsi reached out to ring the doorbell. Emily stopped him. "It would be better if you knocked, dear."

"Oh, right," Pepsi said, and he proceeded to rap twice on the large walnut-stained door.

After a few moments, Rachel Elias answered the door. Standing next to her was a distinguished looking woman of about about seventy.

"Good Shabbos, good Shabbos," Rachel said.

"Good Shabbos," Emily responded.

"Good Shabbos," Pepsi murmured, the words sounding strange on his lips.

"We're so delighted that you've come to join us tonight," Rachel said as she ushered in her guests. She then pointed to her left and said, "Emily, Pepsi, I'd like to introduce you to my mother, Judy Shulman."

"It's so nice to meet you, Mrs. Shulman," Emily said. My husband Joseph and I have heard much about you from Rachel and have been looking forward to meeting you."

"Thank you," Mrs. Shulman responded. "I've heard so much about your family as well. When I heard you would be coming over, I was delighted that Rachel and Daniel asked me to come and move in with them for Shabbos."

"The men and boys are not yet back from shul," Rachel said as she pointed towards the living room. "Please come in and make yourselves comfortable."

As they followed her, Pepsi noticed that the home was filled with an absolutely wonderful aroma. He also saw a lit, six-branched candelabra on the dining room table, and conceded to himself that it made the room look both exquisitely beautiful and somehow deeply spiritual. His mini trance was quickly broken when he felt his pants being tugged just above the knee. It was a pyjama-clad Leah.

She grabbed Pepsi's hand and pulled him towards the couch.

"Come and read to me," she demanded.

After Pepsi sat down, Leah climbed onto his lap. She was holding a large, colorfully illustrated book entitled *The Animals in Noach's Taiva*.

Flipping through a few pages, Pepsi realized that Noach was none other than the biblical Noah, and that *taiva* was the Hebrew word for ark. The object of this particular book seemed to be more about teaching children the various species of animals than the story of the Great Flood.

"You see, Pepsi? Noach is waiting for the Mommy and Daddy bears to go up the ramp on to the taiva."

"How do you know which one is the Mommy and which one is the Daddy?" Pepsi asked.

"You're silly, Pepsi. It's easy shmeezy! The Mommy bear is the one in the pink dress carrying a purse."

Just then the front door opened and the sound of running feet could be heard, as Avi and Dovi sprinted into the living room to see if their famous Shabbos guest had arrived. To Leah's dismay they, too, jumped onto him on the couch.

"Hey, I was here first!" she complained.

"There's room for everybody," Pepsi said, as he picked up a giggling Leah and held her high above his head.

The men entered the room, and Rabbi Elias announced, "Good Shabbos, Emily. Good Shabbos, Pepsi. Thanks so much for coming."

Joseph was wearing a yarmulke, this time a velvet one. Pepsi observed that it was clipped to his father's hair and was sitting stylishly on his head. Rabbi Elias opened a drawer and pulled out a similar-looking one. He held it out to Pepsi. Shedding the children, Pepsi stood up and put it on.

"I hope no one takes a picture of me wearing this," he said, to no one in particular.

"Don't wowwy Pepsi," Dovi said. "Camewas are muktzeh."

"Muktzeh?"

"Muktzeh is the Hebrew word for any object or thing that we don't handle on Shabbos," Rabbi Elias explained. "Money, appliances, even the Shabbos candles themselves. They have to be lit before Shabbos starts, and they must not be moved afterwards."

Rachel interrupted him. "Daniel, I'm sure our guests are hungry. I know I am. There'll be plenty of time for Torah discussion during the meal. Come, let's all move to the dining room and get started."

Pepsi was intrigued by the Shabbos meal. It started with Rabbi Elias and his sons singing a rousing song in Hebrew, followed by him chanting the Kiddush, a blessing recited over a cup of wine, to usher in the Shabbos. Afterwards they all went to perform the ritual of washing their hands for bread. Rachel had given Joe two loaves of home-baked challah bread, and he proudly recited the Hamotzi blessing in Hebrew without assistance. He had studied it with his tutor at the Torah Center that very morning, and it was evident that Joseph was progressing, albeit slowly, in his quest to learn to read Hebrew. The meal itself was delicious, and discussion at the table was wide-ranging. They covered politics—both American and Israeli—and engaged in a spirited debate as to the relative merits of city versus rural living. Rabbi Elias also peppered his sons with questions about the Parsha. The Parsha is a section of the Torah that is recited in shul every Shabbos morning. Each week a new Parsha is read and at that rate, it takes an entire year for the Torah to be completed. The boys were able to answer most of their father's queries, but the one that stumped them generated the most excitement. This was because they were promised a prize if they could come up with the answer before the end of Shabbos.

At first Pepsi could not put his finger on why the dynamics of the Shabbos meal seemed so unusual to him. Then it hit him. For the past hour, there had not been a single interruption or distraction. No one was wearing a communication device. No ring tones—musical or otherwise—and no text message jingles had sounded. The focus of each and everyone at the table was on each other. Pepsi had always recognized that unlike most of his friends, he felt extremely close to his parents and could talk to them. Likely, it was because he was an only child, born to them late in life. But scratching the surface of his consciousness was the thought that if more families would engage in around-the-table, eye-to-eye interaction of the kind he was witnessing tonight, relationships would have a far better chance of succeeding. He wasn't sure how it could be accomplished in the real world, but he conceded that Shabbat somehow, managed to get it done.

Naturally, the conversation drifted to sports. Interestingly, Pepsi discovered that although Rabbi Elias was born and raised in Baltimore, he was a lifelong Yankees fan.

"My grandfather—we called him Zaydie—grew up in New York City. He told me that one summer night when he was five or six years old, after he had already been sent to bed by his mother, his father came in and sat on the edge of his bed. He whispered to him, 'Benjy, how would you like to come into the living room and watch Mickey Mantle hit?' 'Of course,' Benjy said excitedly as he jumped out of bed. On their small black-and-white RCA console TV, he watched Mickey hit a single, and a lifelong Yankees fan was born. He passed along this passion to my father, who passed it on to me. Going to school in Baltimore and rooting for the hated Yankees was tough, but I never wavered in my loyalty, even in the lean years. Naturally the boys are Yankees fans, too. Eli, Dovi, who's your favorite Yankee?"

"Pepsi Meyers!" they answered in unison.

"Well, of all my fans, Eli and Dovi are my favorites," Pepsi responded, to the delight of the boys.

"But you all should know that the biggest Yankees fan sitting at this table is Rachel," Mrs. Shulman said. "Rachel is the youngest of four girls in our family and my late husband treated her like the son he never had. He taught her all he knew about sports, especially baseball."

"I'm not certain I would have married Daniel if he had rooted for anyone else," Rachel said. "We once went to a game at the stadium while we were dating. When he didn't dump me after seeing me cheer and scream like a maniac, I knew we were a match."

Emily turned to Joe and asked him, "Didn't you also tell me your father once woke you up to watch someone hit?"

"It's true. I was five years old at the time. The bases were loaded and Reggie Jackson was the batter. After that, he became my favorite player."

"Do you remember what he did?" Pepsi asked.

"We were all hoping for a grand slam, but instead, Reggie walked. Your Grandpa Howard knew I was disappointed, but he told me, 'Joseph, never forget. A walk is as good as a hit.' Then he sent me back to bed."

"I hope you didn't believe him Dad. We all know it's one of the dumbest baseball phrases ever conceived."

"It is not," countered Joe.

"C'mon, Dad, it makes absolutely no sense!"

What followed was a spirited argument between father and son that, to Rabbi Elias, sounded very much like the give and take that occurs on a regular basis in his Talmud class at the Torah Center.

"I'm sorry to interrupt you guys, but we really should bentch now," Rabbi Elias said. "The boys need to go to sleep. You can pick it up again afterwards over a Grolsch and peanuts in the den."

Bentch is a Yiddish word that means "bless," and the Rabbi was referring to the mitzvah of saying grace after meals. Rachel handed out booklets called bentchers, which contained the text in Hebrew on one side and both an English translation and an English transliteration on the other. The Rabbi and his boys sang the words in Hebrew. Joe and Emily slowly read the transliteration while Pepsi scanned the English translation to discover that much of the prayer had to do with Israel and the Jewish people returning to the rebuilt city of Jerusalem. He did not recite the blessing. Afterwards, everyone pitched in to clear the table, and once the boys had gone to bed, Rabbi Elias retrieved the keg from the fridge and set it up in the den.

Once settled cozily in the den, neither Joe nor Pepsi had the energy to lock horns again, and the conversation drifted to more transcendent matters. Pepsi got it started.

"Rabbi, have you ever seen or heard of anyone who started observing the Torah—and please don't be insulted, Mom and Dad—when they were as old as my folks?"

"A few of my colleagues have had similar experiences, Pepsi," Rabbi Elias said. "Predominantly it is young adults who become BTs. Occasionally parents will be inspired by their children and get on board as well. But the initiative your parents have taken is very, very rare."

Let me jump in here and help everybody out with the terminology. BT is short for Ba'al (m.) Teshuva or Ba'alat (f.) Teshuva, which in Hebrew means a returnee to a Torah-observant lifestyle. A lifelong adherent is called an FFB, which stands for frum from birth. *Frum* (sounds like vroom) is a Yiddish word for someone committed to fulfilling the commandments. Its opposite, *frei* (sounds like fry), refers to someone who prefers freedom and wants no part of any obligatory practices.

"I don't know," Pepsi said. "I feel like I'm too old to even think about a new way of life."

Rachel entered the conversation. "Rabbi Akiva of the Talmud became one of the greatest Jewish sages of all time, yet he only learned how to read

Hebrew at the age of forty. No one should ever say it's too late to learn."

"Rabbi," Joe said. "Maybe you could give Pepsi the short version of your Torah 101 class. I know it made a very strong impression on Emily and me."

"Then I'll need to refill my mug," said the rabbi. "And I strongly recommend that all of you do the same if you're going to survive another one of my boring monologues."

Once everyone had done so, Rabbi Elias commenced. "There are, as you know, many laws and practices required by the Torah. But I think the fundamental principles of Torah Judaism can be distilled into four primary beliefs.

> **One:** A solitary Supreme Being created the universe. We reaffirm this belief every week by observing Shabbat. Shabbat commemorates God's resting on the seventh of what were, a very productive six days.

> **Two:** The aforementioned Supreme Being is aware, interested, and involved in the affairs of man. There is a philosophy that accepts God is the creator, but contends that after fashioning the world He departed the scene. Or, if indeed He is still around watching our affairs, He is a disinterested observer. In other

words, they believe God gave the world a spin to get it started, but once set in motion; He has, and continues to allow, nature and history to run their course. This philosophy is erroneous and is debunked by the saga of the Jewish people's exodus from Egypt. The entire biblical account is an affirmation of an observing and engaged God, and culminates in the splitting of the Red Sea, just as the Jewish people approached it. It remained a pathway to freedom only long enough for the last Israelite to emerge on the other side, after which the waters returned to normal, drowning those intent on keeping the Jewish people enslaved. We reinforce our belief in Divine Providence by performing many mitzvot that commemorate the Exodus. Most notable among them is the holiday of Passover, and in particular, the elaborate rituals of the Seder night.

Three: Seven weeks after departing Egypt, the Jewish people, several million strong, received the Torah directly from God at Mount Sinai. Actually, numbers one and two are not independent of number three. This is because our knowledge and belief in the biblical accounts of Creation and the Exodus, come from the Torah itself. I only mention it as the third fundamental because it is third in chronology.

Four: There is reward and punishment for our deeds. This last fundamental principle presupposes that the Almighty is a loving God who wants to reward us, and that this reckoning takes place on a spiritual level after we depart from this world. At that time we can no longer alter the judgement. This means that the gift of life we all have been granted is a testing ground. It is our opportunity to be virtuous, make proper choices, and please our Maker with the lives we choose to lead.

So there you have it," the Rabbi concluded. "Pretty simple, no? Only four things to remember. Of course you realize I'm kidding. It is anything, but easy."

"But if God truly loves us, as you say," Pepsi asked, "Why did He make following the Torah so difficult and complicated? Wouldn't we be so much more willing and happy to keep its rules and regulations —what you call Mitzvot— if the Torah was easier and less restrictive?"

"Let me throw a question back at you, Pepsi."

"Sure, Rabbi, go ahead."

"What's your batting average?"

"My average?"

"Yup."

"I'm hitting just under .480."

"What if I told you there's a way for you to hit 1.000?"

"I'd say that it's impossible!"

"I'll tell you how it can be done. Whenever you're at bat, we'll take all the defensive players off the field and get the pitcher to lob the ball over the plate. What do you think you'd hit if that happened? I bet you'd never make an out."

"Of course I wouldn't, but it would be meaningless."

"Why?"

"Because the beauty of baseball is in the challenge. To hit a ball that's coming at you at 100 mph while it's spinning and cutting all over the place. When you do that, you feel like a million bucks."

"Well then, Pepsi, wouldn't you agree with me that you've done an extremely good job of answering your own question?"

———•—•———

CHAPTER

6

When You Come To A Fork In The Road, Take It.

Lawrence Peter (Yogi) Berra

The Yankees lost to the Orioles that Friday night, cutting their lead to nine games. Thankfully Pepsi was able to restore order with a triumphant return from his concussion on Saturday afternoon. He hit two home runs and made a spectacular catch in deep left center field, sealing the win for Matthew Slade. Although they lost to Baltimore on Sunday, next up, was a three-game series against the lowly Boston Red Sox, while Baltimore had to play the Western Division–leading Oakland A's. It was shaping up to be a good week for the Bronx Bombers. After the next weekend, the Yankees had extended their lead to 11.5 games. With a mere forty-two games remaining, a familiar swagger had returned to the denizens of the Big Apple. Not that anyone really thought a decade of pathetic incompetence would instill humility in New Yorkers, but their arrogance in thinking nothing could possibly prevent their team from finishing first in the East was breathtaking. They also, could not have been more wrong.

The unraveling began at the top of the third inning of the Thursday night game. It was the first of a four-game series at home against the Houston Astros. With one out and no one on base, Mickey Drake suddenly called time and climbed the steps of the dugout. He stopped briefly to speak with the home plate umpire, and then he limped hurriedly up the third base line, motioning for Mitch Hanks to come towards him. Drake said something to Hanks and then pointed to center field. Hanks immediately began sprinting to the outfield. A puzzled Pepsi stood motionless as his teammate ran straight to him. "Pepsi," Hanks said, breathlessly. "You gotta come in."

"Come in? What's wrong, Mitch?"

"It's your dad. He collapsed at home and they've rushed him to the hospital. There's a police car out front to take you there. That's all I know. I'm so sorry, man. Good luck."

The capacity crowd watched in silence as the young outfielder dropped his glove and took off at full speed towards the infield. As he disappeared down the steps from the dugout into the tunnel, he was met by Melvin Rapp, who was carrying Pepsi's gym bag.

"Come quickly, Pepsi. He's been taken to Columbia Presbyterian in Manhattan. You can change out of your uniform in the patrol car. I'll go with you."

"What happened to him, Mr. Rapp? Was it a heart attack? Is he going to be all right?"

"I'm so sorry, Pepsi, but I really don't know anything. Your mom called my cell from the ambulance and asked me to get you. All she said was that you need to come right away."

As soon as the cruiser pulled away from the curb, the officer activated the siren, and they moved briskly through the congested streets of the Bronx. They made good time over the Macombs Dam Bridge into Manhattan. Pepsi tried calling his mom, but the call went to voice mail. As he changed out of his uniform, Pepsi's mind swirled with dreadful thoughts and emotions and he found himself drawn out of desperation to prayer. *Dear God, if you're truly out there, please, please let my dad be okay. I love him so much and I can't imagine what my mom and I would do if he were to die.* Over and over he repeated those words to himself, until the car came to a screeching stop at the emergency room entrance to the hospital.

Pepsi was quickly escorted through the waiting room to Trauma One. He paled visibly when he caught sight of his father hooked up to a respirator and numerous tubes. Joe was surrounded by a team of doctors and nurses, who were busy attending to him.

"Pepsi, thank God you're here," said Emily as she got up from a chair at the back of the room and rushed into his arms. Her tear-streaked cheeks were blackened by mascara, and Pepsi's heart ached with awareness for the pain and distress he knew she was experiencing.

"Mom, what happened?"

"I don't know. We were watching the game in the living room and your dad got up. He said his back was hurting and he wanted to stretch a bit. A minute later I heard a noise from the kitchen, so I called out to him. When no one answered I went and found him lying on the floor." Emily started sobbing as she said, "I don't understand. He was perfectly fine and then suddenly the very next minute, he was unconscious."

"What do the doctors say, Mom?"

"I'll try my best to answer that for you," said a tall, grey-haired doctor, who was observing the goings-on from the back of the room. "I'm Dr. Henry Stephenson, Chief of Emergency Medicine."

"Thank you. Please tell us, what's wrong with my dad?"

"He apparently suffered a rupture of the abdominal aorta, which is a very serious medical emergency. Likely, he's been walking around with an aneurysm for quite some time without realizing it. I have to be honest with you. Someone who experiences that severe a vascular breakdown rarely makes it to the hospital alive. You can thank the ambulance team for getting him here so quickly. We are doing everything we can to stabilize him, but he's in critical condition and is going to need major surgery. It also will need to be done very soon."

"But he's going to be okay, isn't he?" Pepsi asked.

"It will depend both on the extent of damage to his artery and the severity of his blood loss. We'll only know if we can repair the artery once we go in. But even if it can be repaired, we won't know his status until he regains consciousness."

"Are you saying there is a chance he might not wake up?"

"Unfortunately, the answer is yes. We are concerned about hypovolemic shock and other possible complications. I wish I had better news for you. I'd say his chances of a full recovery are about fifty-fifty."

Emily let out a soft cry as her knees buckled. Pepsi held her tight against him and tried to soothe her by stroking her hair. At that very moment, they heard a nurse call out, "The OR is prepped and ready," and the gurney Joe was on was quickly wheeled from the trauma room to the elevators.

"But I can tell you," Dr. Stephenson continued. "The surgeons here at Columbia Prez are as good as they get. No effort will be spared to give Mr. Meyers the very best care."

They were told on the surgical floor that the procedure would take at least three hours, and an attendant escorted them to a nearby visitors' lounge, which was empty. After settling down, Emily called Marla Holmes. Despite Emily's objections, Marla immediately got in her car to make the drive down from Johnson City to Manhattan. Pepsi called Aunt Sally in Los Angeles. She was so distraught, Pepsi had to ask her to hand the phone to her husband, and he conveyed to Uncle Bill what they knew about Joe's condition. Bill promised to book seats on the red-eye so that he and Sally could be with them in New York the next morning. After hanging up, Pepsi's communicator buzzed. It was a text message from Matthew that read, *If you're up to it, let me know how you're all doing.* Pepsi replied, *Dad's in surgery now. Condition critical, please pray.* A few seconds later came the response, *God Bless.*

"Would you like some company, or would you prefer to be alone?" a familiar voice asked.

It was Daniel Elias. He was standing at the entrance to the lounge with a tray containing four cups of coffee. Rachel was at his side.

"Oh, Rachel, he's so sick," Emily said, tearfully.

Rachel rushed over to Emily and tenderly embraced her.

"How were you able to get in?" Pepsi asked.

"I'm a chaplain here at Columbia," Rabbi Elias said, as he pointed to the hospital pass hanging from his neck. "We just wanted to see how you both were holding up, and if you needed anything."

"Why is this happening, Rabbi?" Pepsi said, with more than a hint of resentment in his voice. "My dad becomes religious and this is how he's rewarded?"

"Pepsi!" Emily said. "Don't talk like that to the rabbi."

"It's all right, Emily. I understand where he's coming from."

"God is watching out for your dad," Emily said. "Until a few days ago we had never heard of Hatzalah, and without them I don't think he would have made it here on time."

"You called Riverdale Hatzalah?" Rachel exclaimed. "They are amazing!"

"Hatzalah?" Pepsi asked.

"Hatzalah is a privately funded volunteer emergency medical response organization that serves various Jewish communities," Rabbi Elias said. "But how did you hear about them, Emily?"

"We received their brochure in the mail a few days ago and Joe read through it," Emily said. "He told me how impressed he was that all the EMTs are volunteers, and he sent them a very nice donation. Then he asked me to put their sticker with the emergency number on the handset in the kitchen. He said, 'You never know when it might come in handy.' That's why I called them. Their ambulance was at our house within minutes."

Pepsi stared at his mother as she spoke. He then turned to Rabbi Elias and said, "I'm sorry for what I said. It's just that I'm so confused I don't know what to think about anything anymore."

"You have nothing to be sorry about, Pepsi," the rabbi replied.

Pepsi stood up and took a cup of coffee from the tray. "Look, I hope you don't get angry with me, but I've given a lot of thought to religion these past few months. I've also spent hours talking with my parents, trying to understand what they see in it. But so much of it makes no sense to me. In fact—and I hope you'll forgive me for saying this Rabbi—but I think the only reason you say you believe in God and Torah is because of your upbringing and education. If you hadn't been raised in a home that preached this way of life, I bet you'd have the same questions I have."

"I do have questions, Pepsi," Rabbi Elias answered softly. "Everyone does, whether they'll admit it or not. But that's not to say there are no answers. And you should know I would never get angry at you or anyone for asking questions. I welcome them. The Torah welcomes them."

"Daniel," Rachel said, "I'm not sure this is the time or place for this kind of discussion."

Emily disagreed. "If Pepsi wants to get something off his chest, now would be as good a time as any. Just sitting here worrying doesn't do anything to help Joe."

"All right, then," Rabbi Elias said. "Go ahead, Pepsi. Shoot."

Pepsi sat down in the chair directly facing the rabbi. "One of the arguments Dad made to me was that in order for things to exist they need to have been designed by a creator. Fair enough. But if that's true, who created God?"

Rabbi Elias nodded. "Anything else?"

"Yes. Why does God allow the wicked to prosper while so many innocent people suffer so much?

The Rabbi nodded.

"One more," Pepsi said. "If the Jewish religion is so great, why have the Jews been the object of so much hate and scorn by the whole world? The little I know about Jewish history is utterly depressing. It's been nothing but century after century of gloom and doom."

Rabbi Elias closed his eyes for a moment and then responded, "First of all, Pepsi, I'd like to disagree with what you said earlier about my belief in God perhaps not being authentic. The truth is I really do believe in God. I truly believe that our people have passed down from generation to generation an authentic account of their experience in the Sinai desert some 3,500 years ago. I absolutely reject the notion that our ancestors lied to their children. I love my children more than anything in the world and I know how much my parents loved me. Why would our forbearers, en masse, deliberately lie to theirs? It is a completely illogical denial of history to maintain that they did so. Christianity and Islam acknowledge the Torah's account of the events at Sinai and accept monotheism as a truism. Where we diverge—and yes, those differences are profound—is not whether there is a Supreme Being or not."

Rabbi Elias paused for a moment to gather his thoughts. "You asked who created God. It's a legitimate question, and I can't imagine any thinking person not having contemplated it at one time or another. It occasionally sneaks into my head through one ear, and never fails to give me a headache before I manage to push it out, through the other. But how does science explain our universe, Pepsi? Science claims that billions of years ago something underwent a chemical or physical reaction, which over eons of time evolved into our multifaceted world. In other words, whatever one thinks about the beginning of the universe, it is uncontested and unanimous that there was some form of something at its very origin that was *not created*. Let scientists contend that this uncreated entity was some kind of sub-atomic particle or primitive micro-organism. I choose to believe that it was God."

A brief smile crossed Pepsi's face as the rabbi's words sank in.

"You asked about the suffering of the righteous or innocent. Welcome to the club! Moses asked the same question of someone much smarter than any of us. He asked it of God. The dialogue is in the Torah, and it is elaborated upon in the Talmud and commentaries. The entire Book of Job is a treatise on this very subject. So you are right—these are legitimate questions. But the answers are found by studying Torah, not running away from it. For your information, the Torah teaches that there is another world after we depart this one, and that is where these apparent injustices will be clarified."

"I don't know, Rabbi," Pepsi said. "You really believe our souls continue living after we die?"

"I do, Pepsi. I think that to believe we are born and we die with no consequence is completely irrational, and demeans the value of life. It would mean that in the end, Mother Teresa's selfless giving and good works gained her nothing more than did Adolf Hitler's life of maniacal genocide."

"But how do you truly believe in something you can't see?"

"You know, Pepsi, I once heard a great rabbi console a mourner with the following story. He said: Try to imagine two twin baby boys having a dialogue in their mother's womb. One of them says, 'Brother, I can't wait until we leave this small, cramped space and move on to a bigger, better world.' The other one replies, 'What are you talking about? This is it, bro. What you see is what you get.' Back and forth they argue, until all of a sudden, the mother's contractions begin and the believing twin exits the womb. The remaining brother is inconsolable. 'My brother has died! I am all alone.' At the very same time the doctor is telling the mother, 'Congratulations! You have a beautiful little baby boy.'" Rabbi Elias paused for a moment to allow Pepsi to absorb the parable. "The Torah teaches that when the righteous and virtuous pass on to the next world, they, too, are received with great joy. And I would venture to say that the difference between the womb and our universe, despite the vastness of the cosmos, pales in comparison to the difference between our universe and the World to Come."

Although his coffee had long ago gone cold, Rabbi Elias took a sip from his paper cup.

"You asked why the Jewish people have suffered so much. Boy, that's a tough one. Not that the question is a deal-breaker, but it most definitely is a painful one to even think about. Truth is, I don't know the answer, and I really don't know anyone who does. But if you think about Jewish history and the extent of the world's animosity towards us, you could ask a better question. You should ask, 'Why are we still here?' For close to two thousand years we had no country to call our own and no ability to defend ourselves. To be a Jew meant living with a mark on our foreheads. Decade after decade we experienced incessant pogroms and forced conversions. We wandered from country to country to find safe haven, but never found it. That is our history in a nutshell. So why didn't we throw in the towel? And you could have asked this question even before a madman named Hitler came along. After enduring the horrors of the Final Solution you'd think every single Jew worldwide would have been waving a white flag and lining up to hand in his birthright. Yet quite the opposite happened, and continues to happen in an absolutely remarkable way. Here in the United States, in Israel, and all over the world. Ask that question of yourself,

Pepsi, and see if you're able to come up with an answer that makes sense."

"I guess we're a pretty stubborn, resilient people, Rabbi," Pepsi said.

"Very true," said Rabbi Elias. "But it also should lead any thinking person to the conclusion that the Jewish people are here to stay, and are destined to play a major role in whatever God's plan is for all mankind."

After glancing at his watch, the Rabbi stood up, and Pepsi followed suit.

"They must be well into the surgery by now," Rabbi Elias said. I feel that I should go down to the chapel to pray a bit."

"Rabbi, wait," Pepsi said. "If you don't mind, I think I'd like to go with you."

Taking the elevator down, Rabbi Elias explained to Pepsi some Torah fundamentals about prayer. "It is important to know that God expects us to ask of Him that which we believe is for the best. That is what prayer is. At the same time, whether our prayer is answered or not, we believe that God does what is best even though we may not understand it. Life, death, success, suffering, war, and peace are but some of the complexities of our world that are beyond our full comprehension. I am telling you this because if your Dad pulls through it does not mean our prayers are what spared him. It may be that in their merit, what we understand to be a harsh judgment was averted. But we will never know for certain. Conversely, if, Heaven forbid, your dad does not make it, it does not mean our prayers were a waste of time and effort. The prayer itself is an affirmation that God is in control. We are obligated, more so in times like these, to make that affirmation."

Pepsi nodded. "What should I say to God?" he asked.

"Express to Him your feelings. Tell Him how much you love your dad, and how much he means to you and your mom. Make a commitment to be a better person, to be a better Jew. But it will have to be sincere, Pepsi, or else...what's the point?"

The Pauline Hartford Memorial Chapel was near the front lobby. Walking down the corridor, they heard intermittent chanting. As they approached, they made out the sound of a solitary voice reciting a verse in Hebrew followed by a response from what sounded like a large assemblage. To Pepsi's surprise, the hallway was jam-packed with people.

"Are prayer services conducted at the hospital all the time?" Pepsi asked.

"Pepsi," Rabbi Elias said. "The only reason these people are here tonight, it to pray for your Dad."

It was an eclectic mix. There were college and Yeshiva students sporting knitted kippahs or black hats on one side, modestly dressed girls and women on the other. Everyone made room for Pepsi to pass through, and as he entered the crowded chapel, Pepsi recognized several people from the Torah Center. Mostly, though, they were complete strangers to him.

"As soon as you left the field the word got out about your father." Rabbi Elias continued. "People from all over the city have been streaming here to show support. And not just from the Jewish community. There's a multi-faith prayer service being held in the next building at the Cofer Memorial Chapel. Fans from all over the city felt they needed to do something."

The man reciting the verses had stopped when Pepsi entered, and there was silence in the room. "Rabbi," Pepsi whispered. "Please thank everyone on my behalf for coming and tell them to please continue."

The rabbi did as requested, and the prayer recital resumed. He then handed Pepsi a yarmulke and a prayer book and pointed him towards a chair in the corner that had been vacated. Pepsi walked over to it and sat down. He lowered his head and began to pray, with the unopened prayer book on his lap.

For close to an hour Pepsi remained deep in thought and virtually motionless. Who knows how much longer he would have stayed like that had he not been interrupted by Rabbi Elias, who, not wishing to disturb the prayers that were ongoing in the chapel, tapped him on the shoulder. He whispered, "I think it's time we went back up to the surgical ward. There might be some news by now, and I think you should be with your mom."

Taking a moment to orient himself, a red-eyed Pepsi looked up at Rabbi Elias and absorbed what he'd been told.

"Yes, of course, Rabbi. Let's go."

As they proceeded back through the hallway to the elevators, Pepsi saw Matthew Slade waiting for him, and they rushed towards each other and embraced.

"Oh man, Pepsi," Matthew said. "I'm so sorry. Do you know anything yet?"

"We're just on our way up to see if they've finished the surgery. Come with us, Matt. Please."

"Are you sure?"

"Of course I'm sure. Mom will be happy to see you. Hey, how'd we do tonight?"

"The Jays clobbered us 11-4. No one could concentrate on baseball. Besides, without you in the line-up, we're a pretty pathetic team."

Pepsi half smiled.

"Don't I know it, my friend. Don't I know it."

Less than an hour after they arrived at the lounge, Dr. Lander, the lead vascular surgeon, strode into the waiting room still wearing his scrubs. He approached Emily. The tension in the room eased dramatically when he pulled down his mask to reveal a broad smile. "The surgery could not have gone better, Mrs. Meyers," he said. "We were able to establish circulation by grafting a medicated aortic stent into place, and the surgical team is closing him up as we speak. I didn't detect any other signs of aneurysm or arterial weakness, so we can be hopeful that this was an isolated occurrence. He will be moved to ICU recovery shortly, where you can see him."

"Are you saying he's out of danger, Doctor?" Pepsi asked.

"His life may be out of danger, but I'm afraid a full recovery is not yet assured. He needs to regain consciousness and display full coherence. We will also have to monitor his kidney function to make sure the loss of blood did not damage them. But his odds of a full recovery have certainly improved dramatically from where they were several hours ago."

Shortly after Emily and Pepsi arrived at the ICU, Joe was wheeled into the room. He seemed to be breathing comfortably, but his complexion was pale and somehow his large stature seemed diminished by the array of machinery and tubes he was connected to. Emily was caressing his hand when she received a text from Marla Holmes that she had arrived and was downstairs in the hospital lobby. Emily wanted to stay, but Pepsi insisted that she not only go down to see Marla, but that she let Marla take her home to Riverdale to get some rest. Emily refused to leave the hospital, but she agreed at least to lay down in the patient lounge as long as Pepsi promised to call her immediately when his dad woke up. She told Pepsi she would send Marla to sleep at the house in Riverdale and bring a change of clothes for both of them early the next morning. After she left, Pepsi positioned a reclining chair at the foot of the bed so that if Joe opened his eyes, he would be the first person Joe saw. Pepsi sat down to his vigil, tilted the chair back a bit, and closed his eyes.

It was the strangest of scenes. Hector Machado and Rabbi Daniel Elias were both standing on different sides of the pitcher's mound firing baseballs at him. "It's not fair!" Pepsi yelled, as he tried to fend off the incoming missiles with his bat. He turned to the umpire as balls were whizzing by his head and said, "Time out! Tell them to stop, please!"

"Sorry, kid," the umpire said. "You can't call for time in the middle of the game."

"Pepsi…Pepsi."

Pepsi awoke with a start. It was his dad whispering his name. Joseph's eyes were open and focused.

"Pepsi," he whispered.

"Dad, you're awake! Thank God."

"What happened? Where am I?"

"Dad, you're in the hospital." Pepsi checked his watch. It was 5:30 in the morning. "You had emergency surgery last night for a ruptured artery."

Pepsi leaned forward and grasped his father's hand. "We were so worried about you, Dad. The doctors weren't sure you'd come out of it."

Joseph winced as he said, "I'm so sorry. I didn't mean to scare you."

"Dad, please. Are you in a lot of pain?"

"Only when I breathe," Joe said with a smile. "Where's your mom?"

Pepsi fumbled for his communicator and called her. She answered on the first ring. "Dad's up! He asked for you. Come on over right away."

A few minutes later Emily arrived at the ICU just as Dr. Lander was making his rounds. "I'm extremely pleased," he announced, after examining Joe and reviewing his chart. "It seems we were able to stabilize Joe before any serious damage occurred. If there are no setbacks, he can be moved out of the ICU this afternoon. I think he's going to be just fine."

When Aunt Sally and Uncle Bill arrived, they joined Emily and Pepsi at Joe's bedside. They were overjoyed to hear the good news about Joe's prognosis.

"Don't you ever do this to me again, brother," she admonished Joe. "The plane ride here was the worst five hours of my life!"

Although Joe kept dozing on and off, the mood in the room was one of relief, and the conversation was light-hearted. At one o'clock a nurse came in and shooed everyone out. After her examination, she told the family that Joe was cleared to be transferred to a private room. An hour later, an orderly arrived to wheel Joe to his new room. In the elevator Joe told Pepsi that he didn't need his son to babysit him.

"Why don't you go to the park, son? Joe whispered. "I'll be fine here with your mother and Sally. Go and help the team. Besides, you always do extremely well against the Blue Jays."

Emily agreed, and when they got to the room, she called Melvin Rapp to arrange for Pepsi to be picked up from the hospital.

Truth be told, although physically exhausted and emotionally drained, Pepsi welcomed the thought of playing ball. What better way to release tension than by turning on a fastball and driving it out of the park? When he arrived at the stadium and entered the locker room to change for batting practice, all his teammates were there. Melvin Rapp and Mickey Drake were also present. They all greeted him warmly and expressed relief that Joe was doing so well. When Pepsi opened his locker, he was surprised to see that his uniform was missing. Even if Rapp had forgotten to bring it back to the park, each player had several uniforms.

"Where's my uniform?" Pepsi asked.

"Pepsi," Mitch Hanks said, holding up a freshly pressed set of pinstripes. "Melvin mentioned to us yesterday that in Hebrew the word life is symbolized by the number eighteen. That's been my number ever since I joined the Yankees. But we all want you to be the one to wear that number from now on. We hope it will be a good luck charm for your dad."

Pepsi had some vague recollection that eighteen was a meaningful number in Judaism, but did not have the faintest idea why. Actually, Torah tradition teaches that every letter in the Hebrew alphabet has a numerical value. The word חי (chai), which in Hebrew means life, is composed of a י (yud) and a ח (chet). Yud being the tenth letter of the alphabet, and chet being the eighth, together they have a value of eighteen.

"I don't know what to say, Mitch. It's really nice of you to do this, but eighteen is your number. I don't want to take it away from you."

"Heck, Pepsi. I was on the Yankees last year and we totally reeked. You're the one who has breathed life into this team. If the number eighteen symbolizes life, no one but you should wear it. Just keep on playing great, and get this team into the playoffs." Hanks handed the uniform to the visibly moved teenager. His teammates then engulfed him, shouting the now-familiar chant of "Pepsi Meyers, Pepsi Meyers, Pepsi Meyers."

Well, Number Eighteen sure breathed some life into the Yankees that night. Pepsi hit a home run and a double, and the Blue Jays were embarrassed by a score of 14-2. In fact, the back page of the *New York Post* the next morning would show a photo of Pepsi in his new uniform under the headline *L'chaim*, with an accompanying article describing the pre-game locker room presentation to the Yankees' young superstar. With the victory secure, Mickey Drake told Pepsi he could skip the last few innings if he wanted to head back to the hospital. Pepsi took advantage of the offer, and after showering and changing, rushed to the hospital to relieve his mom.

"Dad, it's great to see you out of bed!" Pepsi said.

Joe was sitting in a high-back chair at the foot of his bed. A bit of color had returned to his face, and the difference between how he looked now and how he had twenty-four hours before was remarkable. He was wearing his yarmulke, and a small Hebrew/English siddur was resting on his lap.

"Your father even went for a short walk out into the hall," Emily said. "Then he asked to watch the game from the chair."

"Please thank your teammates for me, Pepsi," Joe said. His voice was still weak, and talking was obviously not easy for him, but he continued. "I liked seeing the number eighteen on your back."

Pepsi sat down next to his father and reached out to grasp his hand. "How did you know about the number Dad?" Pepsi asked. "I thought I would be the one to tell you about it, but obviously someone beat me to it."

Joe started to answer, but Emily jumped in and said, "Joseph, you rest." She turned to Pepsi. "Melvin Rapp called before the game and told us about the presentation. He then said that if you are fortunate enough to avoid injury throughout your career, he envisions number eighteen being retired one day and hanging on the wall alongside the numbers of many other Yankee greats. What particularly touched us was that he said not only is he thrilled with your accomplishments on the field, but that your success has helped ignite a sense of pride in being Jewish that he never felt before. Pepsi, it was amazing for your father and me to hear that. There are surely thousands out there who feel just like Mr. Rapp and we can't begin to tell you how proud we are of what you've accomplished."

Joe confirmed Emily's sentiments by squeezing Pepsi's hand just as the nurse entered the room and said, "I'm sorry to break up the party, but it's time you got into bed, Mr. Meyers. I have your meds and a painkiller, so there's no reason you shouldn't be able to get a good night's sleep."

Both she and Pepsi helped Joe get up from the chair and over to the bed. He grimaced in pain as he searched for a comfortable resting position.

"Pepsi, why don't you go home? I'll stay here with your dad tonight," Emily said.

"Nah, Mom. You should go. You've been here all day. You must be exhausted."

"Not a chance, Pepsi. You slept in the chair last night. Tonight it's my turn. Besides, Sally and Bill said they'd come back to relieve me early in the morning. So at worst, I'll take a break then."

"Allright, but I'm not going home. I'll be in the lounge if you need me for any reason."

"Okay. Thank you, son."

Pepsi bent over to kiss Emily on the cheek, and then he leaned over the bed and kissed Joe on the forehead.

"I really hope you and Dad are able to get some sleep."

The couch was uncomfortable and people kept coming in and out of the room, but that was not the reason Pepsi was unable to sleep. His mind could not stop churning over the events, images and emotions of the past twenty four hours.

What does it all mean? How am I supposed to feel now that Dad is out of danger? Can I deny that yesterday I was petrified and at God's mercy, even though—with everything returning to normal—I don't feel that I have any need for Him today? If only life could be as carefree and uncomplicated as baseball. But even being a ballplayer is turning into a burden. How can I be the reason people are feeling pride in their faith…when I don't feel that pride myself? I know almost nothing about our history, our culture, our…Torah. If I start studying it like Mom and Dad, will it change me like it has changed them?

Pepsi continued to toss and turn for another hour or so before exhaustion overtook him and he fell asleep. When he awoke, he rushed over to his father's room to check in on him. As he approached, he could hear laughter. Peering through the open door, he saw his father sitting up in bed with a big smile on his face. Clearly, his uncle and aunt had arrived, and Bill, who was a comedy writer for NBC, was on a roll. Pepsi entered the room. "I'm insulted. You guys are having a party and didn't invite me?"

"Good morning, Pepsi," Emily said. "I checked in on you earlier and you were sleeping like a baby."

"How are you feeling, Dad?"

"I was doing a lot better before Bill got started. My stitches are killing me from laughing too much!"

"The doctor said he could not be more pleased with your father's progress," Emily said. "We really have so much to be thankful for."

"We sure do," Pepsi replied. "Look, I can see that you guys are doing great. So I'm going to head on home to freshen up and maybe catch a few more hours of sleep in a real bed. I'll try to stop by again on the way back to the stadium later this morning."

"Of course, Pepsi," Emily said. "You go on home for now. We'll see you later."

Pepsi went outside and flagged a conventional cab on 165th street. After paying the driver he turned and walked towards his house and stopped. He had seen movement in the Eliases' den window and took a few steps in that direction to get a better look. The blinds were up, and Pepsi could see Rabbi Elias in a T-shirt and shorts jogging on a treadmill. He approached the window, but the rabbi took no notice of him. Pepsi saw that he was engrossed in a Hebrew book that sat on the console of the apparatus. A short while later, the rabbi lifted his head to wipe his brow and was momentarily startled at being observed. Realizing it was Pepsi, he stopped the machine and motioned to meet him out back.

"You're up early today, Pepsi," he said, as he ushered Pepsi from the patio into the kitchen. "Want some coffee?"

"No thanks, Rabbi. I just got here from the hospital and was hoping to sneak in a few hours of shuteye." "How's your dad?"

"It's unbelievable how well he's doing. Isn't life strange? Two nights ago I was sitting in a hospital chapel crying and praying my guts out. Last night, I played baseball."

"It is, indeed."

"You know, my nineteenth birthday is in a few weeks, and I was so afraid my dad would not be around to celebrate it. Now it looks like he'll be back home and things will return to normal. But I don't think I can sweep what just happened under the rug and forget it."

"Of course you can't, Pepsi."

"Rabbi, I listened to your advice the other night and promised God sincerely—I think—that I would try to be a better Jew and that I would somehow find a way to make Torah a part of my life.

But would observing Torah mean I'd have to quit baseball?"

"Nothing in the Torah says you can't play baseball, Pepsi. As long as you don't play on Shabbat or Jewish holidays."

"Playing ball is a violation of the Shabbat?"

"There are different schools of thought as to the propriety of casually playing ball on Shabbat, both in terms of Halacha and with regards to spirit of the day considerations. But I would venture to say that because of the inevitable activation of electronics, playing baseball on Shabbat at the Major League level today would be impossible."

"So you're saying that to be Torah-observant I would have to miss all the Friday night and Saturday afternoon games? That comes out to about one-third of the games played each week. The Yankees would never agree."

Rabbi Elias laughed. "Pepsi, you are by far the best player in all of Major League Baseball. There is no way the Yankees would release you. But if they were dumb enough to do so, every other team in the league would be falling over themselves to sign you, even as a part-time player. I wish I had the job security you do."

"Oh man. What am I supposed to do, Rabbi?"

"What do you mean, Pepsi?"

"The only thing I'm good at is baseball. I just don't see how I can make room for Torah, when baseball is my life."

Rabbi Elias took a moment to wipe his sweaty brow with his towel. "What is baseball, Pepsi?"

"What do you mean, Rabbi? Baseball is a game."

"That's right. Baseball is a game. It's a magnificent game. It's a game of skill, strategy, speed, athleticism, and wonderful unpredictability. In fact it's a sublime game, and you play it better than anyone the world has ever seen. But it's still a game, Pepsi. Life is not a game."

Pepsi had his elbows on his knees, and was rubbing his temples. Rabbi Elias recognized that the young man sitting across from him was experiencing one of those rare moments when the direction of a person's life hangs in the balance.

"Boy, this is going to be tough," Pepsi remarked. "If I start wearing my Jewishness on my sleeve, I'll be ridiculed on the field. Every time I get on base with a single, the opposing team's first baseman is gonna say something like, 'Hey Jew boy. How was your bagel this morning?' Or, 'Better not steal second, Meyers. Everyone's gonna think you're a thieving Jew.'"

"I have no doubt that you're right Pepsi. You'd be navigating difficult territory, and the thickness of your skin would be tested daily. It would also need to be an internal and profoundly private struggle. Not like some players who turn their faith into a theatrical event."

More than likely the rabbi was referring to a slugger in the Los Angeles Dodgers' lineup, who wore a huge gold crucifix around his neck and melodramatically kissed it before each at-bat. Whenever he reached base he would pound his chest and point up towards heaven. Not to mention his interview responses, which were peppered with comments praising his Lord for success on the playing field.

"I'll tell you, though," continued Rabbi Elias, "I think your greatest challenge will come from the fans. Your incredible gift has brought them hope, and hope is addictive. If you miss games and the Yankees start losing without you in the line-up, I'm afraid they might turn against you. It would probably get very nasty, Pepsi."

Pepsi sighed. "If only I weren't Jewish, everything would be so much easier."

"That is true," the Rabbi agreed. "If a Christian ballplayer went to his priest and asked him whether playing ball or leading a spiritual life was a higher calling, I have no doubt that his answer would be the latter. But I would be surprised if he would counsel him not to play on Sunday."

"That's exactly what I mean," Pepsi said.

"Let me tell you a story, Pepsi," Rabbi Elias said. "During the Holocaust, a Jewish couple from Poland begged a Christian woman who was their neighbor, to take in their two-year-old son so he could survive. For four years she raised the boy as her own, and as a Catholic. The boy's parents never returned, having perished in a concentration camp. The Polish woman went to her local priest and asked him to baptize the boy. He told her, 'The child was born Jewish. It is God who decides into which religion someone is born. We have no right to tamper with His choice,' and he refused to perform the rite. Eventually the boy was reunited with his extended family in America, and became a practicing Jew. Pepsi, you're a Jew. You may not have had any choice in the matter, but it's as much a fact of life as is your ability to hit a baseball."

"Okay. I'll do it."

"What did you say?"

"I said I'll do it. My parents were strong enough to make the move, and I'm going to do it, too. Worst thing that can happen is that I'll find out this Torah thing is not for me and I'll say 'oops, sorry…it's all been a big mistake,' and go back to the way I was. But I owe it to my parents and to myself to at least give it a try. I'm not going to let anyone stop me."

I've got to tell you, Rabbi Elias was absolutely stunned. While they were conversing, he thought that at best, after the season and several more months of reflection and study, perhaps there was a chance that Pepsi would take further steps to embrace Torah Judaism. Pepsi's pronouncement that he was actually going to take the leap of faith right now, in the middle of the season, was astonishing.

"From the first moment I saw you swing a bat I've known you were an amazing ballplayer, Pepsi Meyers. But now I can see you're an even more exceptional young man," Rabbi Elias said. "I want you to know that I'm here for you anytime, to help you in any way I can."

"Thank you, Rabbi," Pepsi said as he stood to leave. "I'm sure I'll need it."

Rabbi Elias put his hand on Pepsi's shoulder and walked him to the door. Then he said, "By the way Pepsi do you know who that priest was?"

"No, Rabbi. I never heard the story before."

"It was a young Karol Wojtyła, who would later serve the Catholic Church for twenty-seven years as Pope John Paul II."

———◦•◦———

Shortly after Pepsi went home, Rachel Elias came downstairs to fix herself a cup of coffee. She noticed Daniel sitting at the table with tears in his eyes. "Is everything okay, Daniel?"

"Things couldn't be better, Rachel."

"Then why are you crying?"

"Because I just found out that we have the good fortune to live next door to just about the bravest person in the entire world."

"What happened?"

Daniel proceeded to fill Rachel in on the startling declaration Pepsi had made a few minutes earlier.

"He's going to stop playing on Shabbos altogether?" Rachel asked.

"Yes, he said he would give it a try. You know, Rachel, I'm not certain I understand what happened myself. Had I sensed even the slightest hesitation on his part, I probably would have counseled him to take things slowly and only incrementally increase his Shabbos observance. But you know how different people can be. Some will only enter the water after first dipping their toe in the pool. Others feel the need to jump right in. Pepsi has this relentless intensity about him, which serves him well in baseball, and is now pushing him towards a life of Torah. I sensed it and moved him along in that direction." Daniel paused for a moment and looked at Rachel quizzically. "What? Do you think I should have tried to slow him down?"

"I don't see how you could have, Daniel. All we can do now is wait and see how well the kid can swim."

C H A P T E R

7

If People Don't Want To Come To The Ball Park, How Are You Going To Stop Them?

Lawrence Peter (Yogi) Berra

As you can imagine, the days and weeks that followed were tumultuous. Joseph and Emily welcomed Pepsi's decision with delight. Not so much the New York Yankees. Jason Stern was incredulous when Pepsi broke the news to him, and was not pleased that the task to convey it to Melvin Rapp and the ownership group had been delegated to him. Pepsi chose to face his teammates himself the next day. Reactions ranged from reluctant acceptance to outright anger. What made matters worse was the fact that not only did the Yankees lose the Thursday night game on August 23 to the Blue Jays, but Mitch Hanks severely strained his left hamstring on a routine groundout in the ninth inning and had to be placed on the fifteen-day disabled list.

Actually, there were two things that thoroughly annoyed the Yankee brass. First, they could not believe how utterly stubborn Pepsi proved to be. Melvin Rapp talked himself blue in the face trying to convince Pepsi not to squander his "God-given" talent. Mickey Drake opened his argument to the teenager with a soft-spoken plea for team camaraderie, graduating to an expletive-laced tirade that reverberated deep within the bowels of Yankee Stadium. In both instances, Pepsi hardly responded to their entreaties. He merely advised them that his mind was made up and he had no interest in revisiting his decision. On the other hand, he engaged Matthew Slade at length, trying to explain to his friend what had compelled him to make such life-altering changes. The second matter was their astonishment as to the number of games Pepsi was going to miss. Not only would he be absent for all twelve of the remaining Friday and Saturday games, there were an additional five games that conflicted with the upcoming Jewish holidays. In fact, on August 23rd, at the news conference during which the Yankees made Pepsi's decision public, Mickey Drake expressed his frustration with the following soliloquy:

> "I've got a sister married to a Jewish fella, so it's not like I've never heard of Rosh Hashana. Although, my brother-in-law seems to be fine celebrating only one day of Rosh Hashana, so I'm not really sure why Pepsi has to keep two. As far as Yom Kippur is concerned...well, that's a pretty famous holiday. I think

it's named after some war that happened in Israel a long time ago. But for God's sake, can anyone in this room tell me what the heck Succos is?"

For those of you wondering along with Mickey, Sukkot (also known as Succos), is a holiday during which Jews display their recognition of being under God's protection by setting up booths or huts called sukkot in their backyards or on their porches. Meals are eaten in the sukkah and some people even sleep there for the duration of the holiday. Sukkot is followed by Shmini Atzeret and Simchat Torah. The latter is a day in which Jews celebrate the completion of the yearly cycle of Torah readings in the synagogue. Participants dance for hours with the Torah scrolls, after which the first chapter of Genesis is read aloud and the cycle begins anew.

Drake held up a Yankee schedule to show which days and against which teams his star centerfielder would be off praying or studying while he and the rest of the team were doing their darnedest to make it to the playoffs.

"It's a disaster!" Drake grumbled while pointing at the chart. "Of the remaining thirty seven games left on the schedule, Pepsi is gonna miss seventeen of them. Seventeen!"

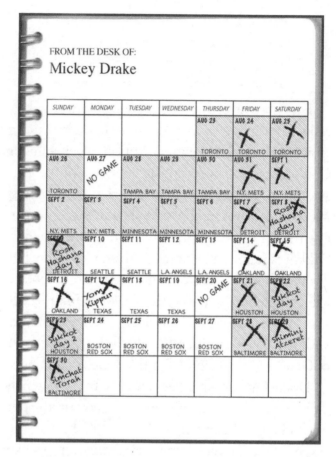

Drake continued. "Don't get me wrong. I got nothing against religion, and I respect the kid's right to do whatever he wants to do with his life. But if he waited this long to find God, I'm sure God won't mind if he waits a few weeks longer. Don't get me wrong. I fully expect our team to make the post-season, with or without Pepsi Meyers in the line-up. For heaven's sake, we've got a 10.5-game lead, and there are only 37 games left to play. So even though Meyers is deep inside my doghouse right now, if we don't make the playoffs, you can blame it on me."

But by the following Monday—after losing three of four to the Jays, and after the Orioles took three of four from the Red Sox—the Yankees' lead had dwindled to 8.5 games. Despite Mickey Drake's bravado, it was Pepsi's head that fans were clamoring for. You see, it wasn't just that he was missing games. All year long, Pepsi's extraordinary exploits had carried over to his teammates. Apparently, the knowledge that he would come through time and again for the team relaxed them. This in turn allowed them to play with an imperiousness that overwhelmed opponents. But that combination of controlled calm and brazen chutzpa had now departed. Players were pressing, and it affected all aspects of their performance. Tang had started swinging for the fences, which was never a good idea. Richardson was suddenly making rookie mistakes. Abraham Jefferson began slumping, and the contagion spread to his twin, Ulysses, who experienced nothing but misery and futility at the plate. Matthew Slade was scuffling because he felt the need to carry the team on his shoulders, which in turn led to control problems that caused him to lose his previous two starts. Even the performance of the great Pepsi Meyers had dipped. Most ballplayers would've killed for the stats he'd had over the previous week, but by his standards Pepsi Meyers was in a slump. Perhaps the smattering of boos that could be heard when his name was announced was affecting him. Regardless, he only managed four hits in twelve official plate appearances, or what would be considered a mere mortal batting average of .333 for that period.

While all of this was happening on the field, Pepsi, in consultation with Rabbi Elias, had commenced his religious training. He was paired with a graduate Yeshiva student named Joshua Roth, who began teaching Pepsi the Hebrew language and basic Jewish rituals. They met each morning, one hour before prayers at the Torah Center. Pepsi learned both how to properly don and make the blessings for tefillin and four-cornered garments with fringes, called tzitzis. After prayers and breakfast, he joined a daily introductory Talmud class given by Rabbi Levi Aaronson, who sported a neatly trimmed beard and spoke with a thick South African accent. Pepsi, one of eighteen students in the class, was pleased that his quest for Jewish knowledge was far from a solitary one. He thoroughly enjoyed discovering the intricate underpinnings of Jewish law and participating in the spirited debate that resounded throughout the classroom. Even on the road, Pepsi kept to his regimen. He video-conferenced with Joshua early each morning, and afterwards, prayed on his own in his hotel room. Matthew Slade had to wear earplugs so that he could sleep undisturbed while his roommate broke his teeth trying to learn the Hebrew language. Pepsi streamed Rabbi Aaronson's Talmud class, and he was able to both follow and participate from all over the country. For Shabbat, Pepsi would leave the hotel and spend the day of rest with a Jewish family from the local community. These arrangements were made by Rabbi Elias back in New York, who had extensive contacts in major urban centers nationwide. Pepsi learned much about Torah-observant neighborhoods across the nation from these weekends, and the synagogues and communities he visited were electrified and energized by the opportunity they had to host the young Yankee phenom.

With the dog days of August and the first week of September in his rear-view mirror, Pepsi was beset with conflicting emotions. He loved studying Torah. He relished the depth of intellectual discourse and was blown away by how much there was to learn and how very little he knew. He discovered that he had the innate discipline to adhere to the daily rituals demanded by the Torah, and he found they suffused his days with a sense of fulfillment. With his father back home from the hospital and rehabilitated, a sense of spiritual calm descended on Pepsi. The first Shabbat when they had walked together to shul was a memory he would always cherish. Though few words passed between them, they each recognized that they were experiencing a moment of father/son bonding of sublime proportions. But the travails of his teammates and the anger being expressed by fans weighed heavily on his mind. The Yankees' ship was leaking oil, and Pepsi Meyers was the one to blame for it. The vitriol expressed towards him by the public who called in to the local sports talk shows was so intense he had to stop listening to the radio altogether. As the Yankees' lead continued to shrink, the catcalling and boos at the stadium grew both in frequency and in intensity. Even though the Yankees were still in position for a playoff berth, attendance dipped precipitously. Many of the fans who continued to show up brought signs to the games expressing their dissatisfaction. Some were creative:

Hey Meyers! Don't You Know GOD is a Yankees Fan?	C'mon Pepsi! You do the PLAYING - We'll do the PRAYING!	I'm Sitting Shiva for the Yankees. Without Pepsi, They're Dead!

Others were crude and sometimes blatantly anti-Semitic, and I won't sully these pages by showing them to you. But kudos to the Yankee Stadium staff, which put an abrupt end to that nonsense by evicting anyone caught displaying an off-color placard. All of this weighed heavily on the kid and made the hours he spent at the ballpark extremely stressful. He was, however, buoyed by a sign he saw in the left field bleachers at the night game on Thursday, September 6. The section was filled with young bearded men in white shirts wearing Yankee caps. They held up a placard that said, CROWN HEIGHTS LOVES PEPSI MEYERS. SHANA TOVA. HAPPY NEW YEAR!

As the Yankees' lead evaporated to four games over Baltimore, the furor over Pepsi's absence from the field grew in intensity. Perhaps the vitriolic comments of fans were to be expected. But the scorn heaped on him by scores of writers and polemicists throughout the country—other than in the Baltimore region—was surprisingly acrid and mean-spirited. For some reason, what this young man chose to do rankled many...even those with little interest in the game of baseball. It was as if they were saying, *How dare anyone forswear the ultimate American Dream in the pursuit of matters of the spirit?* Many even blithely suggested that in their learned opinion, if Pepsi came to the ballpark before Shabbat, playing the game itself on the holy day would not constitute a violation of its sanctity. But in an unusual display of solidarity intended to encourage the teenager, many of the major Jewish organizations from across the spectrum of Torah observance lent their names to the following full-page ad in the *New York Times*:

> We applaud the courage and fortitude of Pepsi Meyers. In the face of criticism and expressions of outrage from across this great nation, he has shown us all that it is possible to place religious and moral principles above all other considerations. He has given honor to the holy day of Shabbat in an unprecedented fashion, and he compels all Jews to ask of themselves, "What am I doing to honor and observe the day chosen by the Creator to be a day of rest for the Jewish people?"
>
> We vigorously dispute the notion that playing the game at the Major League level would not constitute a violation of the Shabbat under Halacha. With the many electronic sensors and cameras constantly activated by player movement, desecration of the Shabbat (Chilul Shabbat) would be unavoidable.

We urge people of good conscience everywhere, to re-evaluate their animus towards this young man. He loves his team and the game of baseball. He has prioritized adherence to the precepts of his ancient but timeless faith, and honors the God of all mankind by doing so.

Somehow through it all, Pepsi was able to persevere. Together with Joseph and Emily, he experienced Rosh Hashana and Yom Kippur for the first time. The solemnity of the Jewish New Year and its striking dissimilarity to its secular counterpart were not lost on the Meyers family. Fasting the entire day of Yom Kippur, difficult as it was to do, felt meaningful and cathartic. Despite their being unfamiliar with the prayers and songs, they thoroughly enjoyed the full day spent in shul. Pepsi wondered as to the propriety of taking up God's time with the fortunes of his baseball team. But he reasoned—when reciting the prayer, *Our Father, our King, inscribe us in the book of income and sustenance*—that he had as much right as anyone to aspire to the economic benefits a World Series ring would bring. Not to mention that if his prayers were answered, he wouldn't have to live with 90% of the residents of New York City absolutely hating his guts. The hectic preparations for Sukkot followed Yom Kippur, and the mitzvah of leaving the comforts of home to live in a temporary dwelling for a number of days fascinated Pepsi. But although Sukkot is to be celebrated with great joy, he felt little but sadness when, upon concluding the afternoon prayers late on September 23, young Avi Elias gave Pepsi the thumbs down. Emilio, the Torah Center's security guard, had been listening to the game and had passed the grim news to Avi. Baltimore had pulled to within one game of the Yankees, with seven left to play.

Mickey Drake called a team meeting before the last Monday night game of the regular season. It was the first of a four-game set against Boston at Fenway. He reminded his troops that they were still a game up on Baltimore, and that while the Orioles were in tough at home against Oakland, the Yankees were playing the Red Sox, the worst team in the league. "I'm telling you, boys," he said. "Oakland will take two of four from Baltimore this week. If we can sweep the Sox, we'll go into the weekend three up, and the O's will have to sweep us just to tie."

Mitch Hanks—who was back in the line-up at slightly less than 100%— laid down the gauntlet for his teammates. "I'm sick and tired of how we've been playing the past few weeks, but I'm even more disgusted that guys in this room have blamed our miserable play on Meyers. We're the ones who've choked, and that's gotta end, tonight." There were murmurs of assent throughout the room. "And as for you," Hanks growled in Pepsi's direction. "You better bring your A game to the park this entire week or I'm personally gonna…"

"I get the picture, Mitch," Pepsi interrupted. "My rabbi essentially told me the same thing this morning. And you guys know by now, I always listen to my rabbi."

Boston never knew what hit them. The greatest of all sport rivalries was, at least this time around, reduced to a one-sided drubbing that would have been agonizing for anyone but a hardboiled Yankees fan to watch. Pepsi Meyers was magnificent. He had fourteen hits in twenty official at-bats, and he took full advantage of Fenway, slugging four home runs to left. He ended the series with a batting average of .462, and his home run total reached forty-five. But what truly broke the hearts of the Red Sox faithful was the Tuesday night pitching performance of Matthew Slade. You see, Matthew spun an absolutely masterful no-hitter—only the twenty-fourth ever tossed by a rookie in Major League history—striking out thirteen and walking but one. And you don't have to be a genius to know what every single Boston fan in the ballpark was thinking while their batters were tossing their helmets and punching the water cooler in frustration. *Matthew Slade was supposed to be a Red Sox.*

Contrary to Drake's prognostication, Baltimore won three of four from the A's, dropping only one game in the standings that week. Entering the final weekend of the season, where they would meet the Yankees head-on in the Bronx, Baltimore had control of its own destiny. Should they win all three games and sweep the series, the O's would prevail and qualify for the post-season. Not the easiest of tasks, mind you. But with the upcoming games scheduled for Friday night, Shabbat afternoon and Sunday afternoon, which would be the Jewish Holiday of Simchat Torah, Pepsi Meyers would not be batting third, nor would he be patrolling center field.

They gave it their all Friday night. In fact, the Yankees broke a 3-3 tie in the bottom of the eighth on a clutch two-out double by Q that drove in Rip Brown from second base. Mickey Drake handed the ball to Heart Attack Jack to close out the game and the division, but he just couldn't do it. He gave up a one-out walk to their number-two hitter. The next batter, Lance Barden turned on a poorly located 95 mph fastball to give the O's the lead. It was an absolutely monstrous 440-foot moonshot well over the back of the Yankees bullpen wall in right center field. Hathaway blew away the Yankees in the bottom of the ninth, striking out two of the three batters he faced for the save. The heartbreaking loss demoralized the Yankees and led to an embarrassing blowout on Saturday. The Orioles, smelling blood, put up crooked numbers in each of the first three innings and cruised to an 11-4 victory. With Meyers unavailable for the Sunday game, the only thing standing in Baltimore's way was the talented arm of young Matthew Slade.

After the game on Saturday night, Melvin Rapp called Mickey Drake to his office to discuss the team roster for the last game of the season. Knowing in advance that Pepsi was going to miss all three weekend games, the Yankees had called up outfielder Aazim Mansouri from AAA to take Pepsi's spot. Mansouri did not play Friday night and only entered the game earlier that day as a defensive substitute, once the dismal outcome had been determined.

"What's the rub, Melvin?" Mickey asked his boss. "We already decided that Mansouri was our best option."

"I'm thinking of maybe driving up to Riverdale tomorrow morning for one more kick at the can. Heck, if I could somehow convince Pepsi to play tomorrow, it would give everyone a lift, especially Slade."

"So you want to know what I think about activating Meyers."

"That's right."

"Go for it, Mel. We already have more players than we need with the expanded roster. I'll make sure to email the League office by the midnight deadline to say he's being reinstated for tomorrow's game. I don't care if you have to get on your hands and knees to beg him. Get the kid to come!"

———•◆•———

CHAPTER

8

Baseball Is Ninety Percent Mental. The Other Half Is Physical.

Lawrence Peter (Yogi) Berra

A chilly, windy morning greeted Joseph and Pepsi as they exited their front door on their way to the Torah Center for the 9:00 AM services that Sunday, the last day of September. Pepsi immediately caught sight of the Yankees' general manager leaning against his car, which was parked right in front of their house on Arlington Street.

"You're wasting your time, Mr. Rapp," Pepsi said to his boss as he and his dad descended the steps to the sidewalk.

Mel ignored the comment and reached out to shake Joe's hand. "It's good to see you up and around, Joe. You're really looking great."

"Thanks, Melvin. I feel very blessed, considering what kind of shape I was in a few weeks ago."

"That's nice to hear. Look, I'm not going to beat around the bush. Pepsi, we need you to play for us today. Everyone has been patient and gracious towards you, kid. The ownership group, management, your teammates, even most of the fans have cut you a lot of slack. But our backs are to the wall, and without you, I don't think we're gonna make it. There's a lot of self-doubt in the locker room, and if we fall short, I can't imagine that your teammates—even Matthew—would ever forgive you for letting that happen to them. I know that I won't be able to. Don't get me wrong. I admire what you're doing and in some ways I envy your idealism. But, Pepsi, your road to spiritual fulfillment is being paved over an awful lot of broken hearts."

Joe was not particularly pleased with Melvin Rapp for ambushing them on the way to shul. "I'm surprised at you, Melvin. Are you so disenfranchised from your heritage that you could possibly think a baseball game is more significant than Simchat Torah?"

"C'mon, Joe. You know I have the utmost respect for the Jewish faith. One of my favorite players of all time—and he retired from the game well before I was born—is Sandy Koufax. Not only because he was the greatest Jewish pitcher of all time, but because he refused to pitch on Yom Kippur. But for heaven's sake, Sandy only shut it down for one day and was not an everyday player. What I'm actually trying to do is protect Pepsi. Think about it. Is there a team in the league with a stronger sense of tradition and pride than the Yankees? If we lose, it will go down as one of the worst and most embarrassing chokes in the history of the franchise, even worse than losing four straight to Boston back at the turn of the century. You don't want that to be Pepsi's legacy, do you?"

Joe shook his head emphatically and pointed his finger at Rapp. "You talk about Yankee tradition. What is it altogether, 150 years old? How about a 3,500-year-old tradition that laid the foundation and the code of conduct for our people, if not the entire human race? Baseball has absolutely no place at the table when it comes to Torah. You really should know better, Melvin."

"I have to agree with my dad," Pepsi said. "If anyone should be trying to convince the other to have a change of heart, it should be us getting you to come to shul with us. We danced for hours last night and it was beautiful and I'm going to try my best to do it all over again today. Sure I'll be thinking about my teammates and I empathize with the fans, but if we don't win and move on, I'll be able to live with it."

Melvin Rapp did not respond. He watched Pepsi and Joe as they turned and headed down the block towards the Torah Center. It was a good several minutes before he could be observed shaking his head as he got into his car and drove off.

The joy that permeates a synagogue annually on Simchat Torah is difficult to describe. It is more than just the elation of having finished reading the entire Torah and the anticipation of starting it anew.

It is the day on which Jews who feel connected to the Torah express their love and reverence for the laws and lessons contained in it. They recognize it as a divine gift through which they may achieve a fulfilling and meaningful life, and they relish the once-a-year opportunity to sing and dance the day away while clutching the Torah scrolls close to their hearts. It is also a day of festive eating and drinking. The pre-holiday classes Pepsi Meyers had attended had whetted his appetite for the celebration, and several of his new classmates, who had participated in years prior, spoke of Simchat Torah as a unique fusion of sensory and spiritual pleasure they had never experienced elsewhere. But though he went through the motions, Pepsi circled the synagogue carrying the Torah with a heavy heart. His encounter with Rapp and the guilt he felt about his team, his friends, and especially Matthew, wore him down. His mood matched the weather of that blustery and unseasonably cold early October day. Charcoal grey clouds were billowing in from the west, carrying with them a sense of gloom.

A powerful but brief thunderstorm rumbled through the Bronx fifteen minutes before the early afternoon game was scheduled to start, and the Yankee Stadium grounds crew had to scramble furiously to get the tarp on the infield. It only lasted twenty minutes, after which clear skies returned, bathing the stadium in brilliant sunlight. A bit more than an hour after the game's scheduled start, the Oriole's leadoff man settled into the batter's box, and to the impatient crowd's delight, the umpire bellowed, "Play ball!"

It was a baseball purist's dream come true. The pitcher's duel had Yankees and Orioles fans on the edge of their seats from the opening pitch. Slade and his opponent, a twenty-five-year-old named Devon Gooden, (a great grandson of New York Mets legend, Dwight Gooden) were clearly in top form. Furthermore, a strong wind was blowing in from right field. When Ting Tang absolutely crushed a ball to right center in the bottom of the fourth, it died on the warning track to the chagrin of the 49,000 fans in attendance and of Yankees supporters around the world. Slade was magnificent. Mixing his fastball and slider while masterfully varying the speed of his pitches, he had the Orioles completely off balance. Matthew used Joseph's calming techniques and felt utterly at ease on the mound. Baltimore had yet to hit a ball hard, and they had managed only one infield single in the third and an excuse-me Texas League double in the sixth. Nevertheless, the tension was unbearable as the Yankees, too, failed to break through against Gooden. That is, until Roger Dawson came to bat with two out in the bottom of the seventh. After fouling off several tough pitches, Roger managed to hit a sinking line drive that Shannon Brooke, the Orioles' Gold Glove centerfielder, should have played on one hop. Instead, he attempted a shoestring catch and the ball skipped by him, rolling towards the warning track in straightaway center. Dawson turned on the jets and was well past second base by the time Brooke retrieved the ball. Seeing that Brooke's throw to shortstop was going to be accurate, the Yankees' third base coach put up the stop sign to hold Dawson to a triple, but the speedy Jamaican ran right through it. The shortstop's relay to home was slightly up the first base line, and that was all Dawson needed. With a head-first slide, his hand touched the plate just before he was tagged on the elbow.

"Safe!" was the umpire's emphatic call. When the ruling was corroborated by the word *Safe* flashing on the scoreboard, Yankee Stadium erupted in joyous exaltation. Meanwhile a few miles to the north at the Riverdale Torah Center, with his wireless ear bud tuned to the ballgame, Emilio pumped his fist and mumbled "Vamanos Yanquis" under his breath.

When Matthew Slade took the mound in the top of the eighth, the short porch fans behind the right field wall started calling out his name. Before long the surrounding sections joined in, and soon a groundswell had Yankee fans throughout the Stadium on their feet chanting, "Matthew Slade! Matthew Slade! Matthew Slade!" It continued as he let fly the first pitch of the inning, a lightning-fast bullet on the inside corner that was called a strike by the umpire. It grew louder when the batter flailed away at the second pitch, managing only to dribble it foul towards the on-deck circle. The noise level intensified when Matthew broke off an exquisitely shaped curveball that completely froze the Orioles' batter, as it grazed the outer edge of the plate. "Strike three," barked the umpire, while the Matthew Slade chant continued unabated throughout the park.

Broderick Schmidt of ESPN was doing his best to describe the scene. "The noise is deafening and the stadium is shaking! Yankee fans in unison have risen to their feet as if to will their beloved rookie pitcher to victory, and it seems to be working."

"Strike one!" cried the umpire, as the first pitch to the second batter impacted Rip Brown's mitt behind the plate.

Matthew Slade! Matthew Slade! Matthew Slade!

"Strike two!" bellowed the ump, as the intimidated batter once again failed to pull the trigger on Slade's 105 mph fastball.

Working fast, Matthew acknowledged his catcher's sign and released, with the very same arm motion as for his fastball, an 87 mph change-up. Utterly fooled, the batter's optimistic swing came to an end with the ball still more than five feet from home plate, prompting the decibel level in the arena to continue its climb into uncharted territory. The umpire called, "Strike three!"

Matthew Slade! Matthew Slade! Matthew Slade!

Wouldn't you know it, Baltimore's third batter of the inning fared no better than his compatriots had, and when he, too, failed to make contact with the third pitch thrown to him, the Stadium erupted.

MATTHEW SLADE! MATTHEW SLADE! MATTHEW SLADE!

In the booth, Sam Weller could barely contain himself. "Broderick, do you realize what just happened?"

Schmidt was only too happy to take the cue. "Matthew Slade, ladies and gentlemen, has just pitched what is known as an immaculate inning. With only nine pitches, he struck out three batters. It is an extremely rare feat, and I'm told that in all of Major League history it has never before been accomplished by a rookie. And to think that Matthew Slade did it in the most important and pressure-filled game of the year for his team. Amazing...absolutely, undeniably amazing."

MATTHEW SLADE! MATTHEW SLADE!
MATTHEW SLADE!

With his heart pounding furiously in his chest, Matthew descended the mound and walked towards the Yankee dugout, all the while thinking, *One more inning—all you need to do is hold it together for one more inning.* But just as he tipped his cap to the roaring crowd, a terrifying bolt of lightning streaked across the sky, followed by a booming clap of thunder that shook the stadium and silenced the crowd. The ensuing raindrops quickly turned into a torrential downpour that prompted the umpires to call time and the fans to scurry for cover.

There was no way the umpires were going to terminate a game of this magnitude —certainly not when the score was only 1-0 — and award the Yankees a rain-shortened victory, especially since it was predicted that the storm cell would only take two hours to pass, and that clear skies were to follow for the rest of the evening. Because of the delay, both teams would have to replace their starters. Baltimore was hoping, of course, that its bullpen would shut down the Yankees in the bottom of the eighth and that they could somehow scratch out a run or two against Jack McBride in the top of the ninth.

The last dance with the Torah scrolls, as they were lovingly returned to the Holy Ark, was a sight to behold. Rabbi Elias and several of the Torah Center's leading members danced with the Torahs through a long row of worshippers, who stood opposite each other with their hands clasped high above their heads to create an aisle and a canopy for them to pass through. The shul was shaking from the combination of joyous singing and stomping feet. Emily took in the exuberant scene from her vantage point in the balcony. She particularly enjoyed watching her husband and son as they stood fronting each other with clasped hands as the Torahs passed between them. Their faces exuded contentment and a sense of belonging, a feeling that was washing over her as well.

Once the scrolls were put away, Mussaf prayers were recited, after which the Torah Center hosted a late lunch in the social hall for its entire membership. It was one of the highlights of the year for this segment of the Riverdale Jewish community. In addition to a luxuriously catered meal and spirited singing, various members presented thought-provoking words that focused on the laws and significance of Simchat Torah. Rabbi Elias implored his congregation to strive to maintain the spiritual levels achieved during the Days of Awe and the holiday season in the winter months ahead. About halfway through his sermon, the rabbi's speech was interrupted by a loud crash of thunder, a momentary power outage, and the unmistakable sound and scent of vigorous rainfall. For some reason, the significance of the inclement weather completely flew over Pepsi's head. Not so Joseph Meyers. He immediately looked at his watch and calculated that if the game had not been concluded before the storm and the delay of game was lengthy, Pepsi might still be able to impact its outcome. He got up from his chair to check the almanac hanging in the hallway. The holiday would end at 7:15 PM, which was less than two hours away.

Watching the steady rain from his office window, Melvin Rapp had the very same notion. He called down to the clubhouse and asked to speak with Matthew, but was told he was in the shower. He left a message that Slade should come and see him in his office right away. About fifteen minutes later, there was a knock on his door.

"Come in, Matt…and please close the door behind you."

"What is it, Mr. Rapp?"

"First of all, I want you know how proud we are of you. You gave us one the greatest clutch pitching performances in Yankees history this afternoon. And I'm sure that if not for the weather you'd have finished off Baltimore in the ninth, and we'd already be drinking champagne."

"Thank you. I just hope we'll be able to hang on."

"Well, that's the thing. We've been told that the rain will last close to two hours. That means by the time we're back on the field, the Jewish holiday will be over, and Pepsi will be able to come to the park and suit up."

"Pepsi's on the roster?"

"Mickey emailed the commissioner's office just in time last night to put him on. I thought if I went to see him in Riverdale this morning I'd somehow be able to convince him to forget about the holiday and play. Obviously that didn't work out as well as I thought it would."

"I could have saved you the trip. There were better odds of Rip Brown hitting an inside-the-park home run than of you getting that stubborn mule Meyers to change his mind."

"Yeah, I guess you're right. But let's at least get him down here right after dark. He might yet be able to play the last inning. More if it goes to extras."

"So, you want me to go up to Riverdale and get him over here, right?"

"That's exactly what I'd like you to do, Matt. I've alerted the driver to get the limousine ready. Take it up to Riverdale and get him out of there as fast as you can after 7:15. Bring along his uniform so he can change on the way down and try to get him pumped. I'll do what I can over here to stall the resumption of play as long as possible."

"I got it, boss. Piece of cake."

———•·•———

Although the tall figure of Matthew Slade standing in the hallway outside the sanctuary of the Jewish Center was certainly incongruous, a degree in rocket science was unnecessary to realize why he was there. Pepsi was already inside the sanctuary for the final evening prayer when Matt arrived, but word had spread about the visitor. When Pepsi took the three backward steps after finishing the Amidah of the evening prayer, Avi Elias whispered in his ear that the game had been delayed by rain, and that his friend was waiting for him in the hall. Pepsi, seeing that Rabbi Elias had also concluded his prayers, rushed over to him to ask him what to do. The rabbi quickly ushered Pepsi into his study, pulled out a bottle of wine and a silver cup, and recited the Havdalah, a blessing to signify the end of the holiday.

"Now you can go, Pepsi. Get there as fast as you can. And of course, best of luck!"

Pepsi's dash back through the shul towards the hallway was accompanied by exhortations from many of the congregants. "Go get 'em Pepsi!" "You can do it!" "Make us proud!"

When Pepsi burst into the hallway, Matthew grabbed him. They rushed out to the limo, which took off for Yankee Stadium with a shrill squeal of tires. A hologram broadcast of the game was visible on the glass partition behind the driver, and it was immediately clear that the game had yet to resume. Yankees' announcer Tommy Deloraine was commenting that in all his years in the booth, he'd never seen the grounds crew have so much difficulty rolling up the tarpaulin that covered the infield. He then proceeded to describe an animated on-field argument between Mickey Drake and the chief of the umpiring crew. "I don't know what the delay is, ladies and gentlemen. Baltimore's been on the field for several minutes, and their pitcher is all done with his warm-ups. Home plate umpire, Sal Bernadini, is barking at Drake and emphatically pointing to the batter's box. So it seems like he's telling Drake to get his hitter up, and for some reason Mickey doesn't want to do that. Okay, finally. Drake is slowly heading towards the dugout, and I can see that Max Durning has grabbed a bat and a rag of pine tar."

"Tell me all about the last two games, Matt," Pepsi said, unbuttoning his shirt.

"We lost a tough one on Friday night. We were up 4-3 late, but Barden turned on McBride for a two-run shot in the top of the ninth."

"What did he throw him?"

"Fastball."

On the air, Deloraine was saying, "Durning hits a high fly ball to center field. It's an easy play for Shannon Brooke, and he puts it away for the first out."

Pepsi wiggled out of his suit jacket as Slade continued. "We were never in the game yesterday and got blown out, but today I managed to shut them out through eight. That's when the rain came. Roger hit an inside-the-parker. You should have seen him fly. But we're only up 1-0. Man, it's good to have you back."

"Wow, great job Matt," Pepsi said as he untucked and removed his shirt, revealing a four-cornered garment with strings attached to each corner underneath.

"Dawson pops it up in the infield," Deloraine said. "That's an easy play for the first baseman. There are now two gone in the bottom of the eighth."

After maneuvering himself into his uniform, Pepsi took off his dress socks and exchanged them for white crews, over which he donned long black stirrups that reached just below the knees.

"Who's coming up for Baltimore in the top of the ninth?" Pepsi asked his friend.

"At least there's some good news there. It's seven through nine. Not likely that Barden will get to hit."

Deloraine could be heard shouting. "Quinteria lines a base hit to left center field. Brooke races over to cut it off and backhands it in the gap."

Pepsi and Matthew both turned towards the glass to watch as the play developed.

"Quinteria is trying for second. Brooke fires the ball as Quintera slides in head first. It's going to be close. Heeeeee's OUT! What a great play by Brooke to end the eighth. So now the intrigue continues and the drama intensifies as we wait to see if the erratic Jack McBride can come in and save the season for the Yankees. Stay tuned, everybody. We'll be right back."

"Excuse me, driver," Matthew said. "Are we almost there?"

"We'll be there in less than a minute, sir. It's just around the corner."

Matthew quickly called Melvin Rapp, who answered on the first ring.

"The driver says we're a minute away Mel. Have Mickey make the line-up change with the ump. Don't worry. I'll get him there in time."

As McBride tossed his warmup pitches, the familiar voice of the Yankee public address announcer rang out through the stadium, only this time, a bit more languidly than usual.

"*Ladies and gentlemen, now pitching for the New York Yankees, number fifty-four, Jack McBride. Now playing right field for the New York Yankees, number forty-one, Ulysses Jefferson.*"

At that moment, a familiar figure emerged from the dugout on the first base side of the field, and sprinted across the diamond.

"*Now playing center field for the New York Yankees, number eighteen, Pepsi Meyers.*"

With the last announcement, a buzz spread through the crowd. Mostly there was enthusiastic applause, but a smattering of boos and jeers could also be heard. Both died down quickly when the game resumed. The precarious lead held by the Yankees offered little comfort to the fans, and the tension in the air was palpable. McBride had succeeded in closing thirty-nine games up to that point in the season, but he had blown seven, most recently the Friday night game against Baltimore. So when his 98 mph fastball on the outside corner was called strike one, Yankee fans allowed themselves to exhale, hoping that their closer would seal the deal without incident. When the next pitch resulted in a soft groundout to second, their optimism continued to grow, as did the noise level throughout the stadium. Pepsi was relieved that the first play took place in the infield. He was using every spare moment between batters and pitches to warm up and stretch. Batter number two fared no better than the first. McBride was sharp with both his fastball and slider, and took only four pitches to strike out the Orioles' number-eight hitter. By this time, everyone attending the game was on their feet. Even the vendors had stopped hawking their wares, pausing—if only for a moment—to become Yankee fans again. And they, along with all Yankee fans everywhere, were urging, willing, and indeed praying to any higher power that might be listening, for McBride to get one more out.

Ladies and gentlemen, now batting for Baltimore, number seventy-seven, Emmanuel Mokbuma. Mokbuma, the first Nigerian ever to play Major League Baseball, was an athletic and powerful right-handed hitter, who had slugged three pinch-hit home runs that year. Rarely used against right-handed pitchers, Baltimore's manager was rolling the dice by pinch hitting him, hoping that he would run into one against McBride and tie up the game. The first pitch from Heart Attack Jack was a crisp slider on the inside corner that Mokbuma swung at mightily. He managed to only nick the top of the ball and sent a soft, slow roller with just enough energy to travel about halfway up the third base line. Mitch Hanks, who was playing deep, charged in quickly, but immediately realized he would not have time to throw out the swift Mokbuma at first. His only play was to allow the ball to roll foul. Agonizingly, the ball rolled off the grass onto the dirt portion of the infield. To the chagrin of Yankees fans, the ball seemed to defy nature by running out of topspin and coming to a stop right on the chalk line. "Fair ball!" shouted the third base ump, long after Mokbuma had crossed first base on the other side of the infield.

I'm not sure why, but enthusiasm doesn't seem to go along with sweaty palms. Yankee Stadium, which a moment before was pulsating with noise and optimism, now produced only a dull murmur. Was McBride's rotten luck an omen of things to come? Baltimore's leadoff man, the swift and dangerous Mackey Rohr, was coming to bat, and with Mokbuma's speed, an extra base hit could very well tie the game. An audible gasp could be heard coming from the stands when Rohr laced the third pitch he saw from McBride deep into the right field corner. Off the bat it looked like it might leave the park, but fortunately for the Yanks, it bounced high off the wall right into Ulysses Jefferson's glove. His throw to the cut-off man was on the money, and though Mokbuma was off at the crack of the bat, he had no choice but to hold up at third base. Meanwhile, Rohr easily cruised into second with a stand-up double. The next batter, right hand-ed-hitting Shannon Brooke, could propel his team into the lead with a base hit. Sadly for the Yankees, it was something he excelled at doing. Brooke was among the league leaders in hits, on-base per-centage, and batting average with men in scoring position. McBride had no choice but to pitch to Brooke. On deck was Lance Barden, the leading home run and run-producing player in the game. He also sported a .450 lifetime batting average against Heart Attack Jack.

Rip Brown signaled for an inside slider, and McBride nodded. After checking the runners, he let the pitch fly directly towards Brooke's left hip. At the last moment, the ball began to curve sharply away from the batter towards the inside corner. Apparently, though, as it passed Brooke and settled into the catcher's mitt, it grazed his uniform and generated an audible click by nicking the button of his shirt right above the belt. Brooke immediately turned to the umpire and pointed to his uniform.

"Time!" yelled the home plate umpire as he raised his hands high into the air. He motioned Brooke towards first base, indicating that he'd been hit by the pitch. McBride lost it.

"That ball was a strike!" he screamed. "Brooke leaned over the inside corner. How can you send him to first?"

Rip Brown was apoplectic as well. Flinging his helmet aside, he put his face right up against the umpire's mask and expressed his displeasure audibly enough for the network microphones to catch it all.

"What's wrong with you Bernadini? Are you blind…or just dumb? This has got to be the worst, most gutless call in the history of baseball!"

Mickey Drake hadn't moved so fast in years. He could ill afford to have his closer and catcher thrown out of the game, and he sprinted from the dugout to get between his players and the umpire.

"Sal," Mickey said, pushing Brown away. "You can reverse this. Go consult with the other umps and ask them what they think. This game's too big to be decided like this."

"Go back to the dugout, Mickey. I've made my call. If you stay out here and embarrass me, I'll have no choice but to toss you."

"C'mon, Sal, you're killing me. Show some courage and confer about this. Brooke made no attempt to get out of the way. No attempt at all."

Fans in the stands were on their feet booing and hurling invectives at Bernadini as only New Yorkers can. Meanwhile the network's sound editors were busy trying to keep the expletives from making it into living rooms all across the globe.

"I'm warning you, Mickey. Get back to the dugout now or you're gone."

"You're an embarrassment to the game, Sal. You're spineless and clueless and I'm gonna make it my mission in life to get you out of baseball!"

"You're outta here!" Bernadini shouted, as he thrust out his arm and pointed his finger towards the Yankees' dugout.

Drake threw his cap down and with hands on hips, moved his face inches from Bernadini's. He then yelled loud enough for all the fans behind home plate to hear, "You're the one who should be tossed, you pathetic jerk."

Bernadini turned away from Drake, and the three other umpires jumped in to block the incensed manager from following him, angling Drake towards the Yankees' dugout. The crowd escalated their expression of displeasure by raining down on the field anything and everything they could get their hands on. Beer cups—empty and otherwise—as well as scorecards and food of all kinds, were sent hurtling through the air. More dangerously, foul balls hit earlier into the stands were being launched at the umpires, who scurried into the dugout to get out of harm's way. To no one's surprise, within a few short moments the public address announcer declared:

"Ladies and gentlemen, please refrain from throwing anything onto the field of play. We have been advised by the office of the commissioner of baseball that if this behavior does not cease immediately, the game will be forfeited, and the Baltimore Orioles will be declared winners of both this contest and of the American League Eastern Division."

Although the announcement was met with boos and catcalls, the fans were prudent enough to stow away their projectiles, and after a few moments, the umpires returned to the playing field.

It sounded like it started with a lone voice sitting behind the Yankee dugout, but it quickly spread from row to row and section to section throughout the stadium. At the end, there were more than fifty thousand New Yorkers chanting simultaneously in perfect unison, "toss the ump, toss the ump!" This went on for about half a minute, only to subside when Lance Barden was announced and started walking towards the batter's box. The chanting further abated as the slugger banged his bat against his cleats and refastened the Velcro straps on his batting gloves. By the time he dug in and lifted his head to glare at McBride, the arena was virtually silent. This was because every fan in Yankee stadium instinctively knew that in all likelihood, the final act of their beloved team's dramatic roller coaster season was about to unfold.

Outfielders are expected to read the scouting reports of opposing hitters and know where to place themselves on the field. A team's bench coach will assist them in this task and motion to them from the dugout if they're out of position. Lance Barden was an anomaly. He would and could hit the ball anywhere. His spray chart, whether batting lefty or righty, was uncannily uniform across the board. Right, center, left, it didn't matter. He hit the ball no matter where it was pitched, and it was your good fortune if you just happened to be there to catch it. In this situation, all the outfielders had to play deep. If Barden dropped a hit in front of any one of them, Baltimore would score two runs and take the lead. But if he hit one over their heads, the O's would easily score three, making a comeback in the bottom of the inning very unlikely.

Pepsi could feel the adrenaline surging through his bloodstream as McBride readied himself to release the first pitch. Bouncing on the balls of his feet to stay loose, he peered in and saw that Rip Brown had called for a slider away. Pepsi's eyesight gave him a huge advantage over his teammates, who could not clearly see from the outfield what was being called, or precisely where the catcher was setting his target. With this knowledge, Pepsi shifted a few steps towards left field, where Barden, hitting left-handed, would be more likely to hit an outside pitch. McBride's slider started well outside the zone but broke sharply towards the vicinity of the outside corner. Barden thought it was wide and did not swing at it. To the crowd's delight, Bernadini disagreed and forcefully declared it to be strike one. Brown called for another slider, this time down and in, and once again Pepsi adjusted his position, moving several strides to his left and towards right field. This time the pitch seemed to be heading straight down the middle, but it broke late towards the inside corner. Once again Barden took the pitch, and once again Bernadini hollered, "That's on the corner. Strike two!" Barden turned to glare at the umpire, thinking to himself that Bernadini was doing his best to make amends for the admittedly lousy call he had made in favor of Shannon Brooke. He also resolved that if the next pitch was anywhere near the strike zone, he'd have no choice but to swing at it.

C'mon Rip, Pepsi thought to himself. Think it through! Barden's gonna be sitting on the slider. He knows after burning you Friday night you'll be afraid to call for a fastball. Not to mention that Jack has just thrown two of the best sliders of his career. But I beg of you, please, don't do it. If Jack throws one more slider,

Barden will knock it out of the park. Call for the heater. It's the only way to get him out.

I can't begin to tell you how relieved Pepsi was to see Rip Brown pointing to the ground with a solitary index finger, and wagging it towards his left side, indicating a fastball away. Pepsi took a few steps to his right, and a few steps in towards the infield. McBride, from the stretch, began his motion. Pepsi took another step to his right and one more step in. *There's no way he can get around on the fastball. He's sitting slider.* McBride released the ball, and Pepsi could see immediately that it was heading towards the upper quadrant of the outside corner of the strike zone. He accelerated his movements, both forward and to his right. *Barden has no choice but to swing at it, and he's going to be late. At best he'll hit it off the end of the bat.*

I would venture to say that just about all New Yorkers (even Mets fans) were tuned in to the game that Sunday night. Millions were in their homes, eyes glued to their oversized television sets. Most people out and about had stopped whatever they were doing to follow the game on their mobile devices. Thousands more were standing in Times Square viewing the huge monitor on the Times Tower. Cabbies and anyone else driving their cars at the moment had the privilege of hearing Tommy

Deloraine's call, which was being simulcast on local and satellite radio.

"Barden swings and hits a soft, looping line drive over short. Quinteria is racing towards the outfield with his glove outstretched. I don't think he can reach it. The ball is going to fall in for a...wait a minute...PEPSI MEYERS MAKES A HEAD-FIRST DIVE! The ball is sitting like a snow cone in the webbing of his glove, but I don't know if he caught it or trapped it. The Orioles are circling the bases, but there's been no indication, no signal from the second base umpire. He's obviously unsure, and doesn't want to make the call."

Fans of both teams held their breath as what seemed like an interminable five seconds ticked off between the end of the play and the AUTO-UMP ruling.

BATTER IS OUT. BATTER IS OUT.

Deloraine exploded. "He caught the ball! He caught the ball! Pepsi Meyers came out of nowhere and caught the ball! The game is over and the New York Yankees are going to the playoffs! Yankee players from all over the field, dugout and bull-pen are sprinting out to short center field. They're piling on top of Pepsi Meyers in jubilation. Wait a minute...there are fans, hundreds of fans pour-ing on to the field as well. My, oh my. They've overwhelmed security and are swarming towards the outfield, where Pepsi and his teammates have gathered. There is chaos in the Bronx, ladies and gentlemen. And I'm loving every minute of it!"

The video replay of the catch revealed precisely how remarkable it was. The center field isolation camera showed that Pepsi had started running towards the infield while the ball was still on its way to home plate. After Barden made contact, Pepsi accelerated into an all-out sprint, his cap flying off in one direction, the yarmulke beneath it in another. His desperate lunge for the ball, after it had sailed over Quinteria's outstretched glove, ended its downward trajectory a mere inch from the top of the grass. With the ball half in and half out of his glove's webbing, Pepsi's face slammed into the soggy turf, and he slid for several yards on the slick grass. After coming to a stop, he remained motionless until the AUTO-UMP announcement. He then rolled onto his back, transferred the ball from his glove to his bare hand, and pumped it in the air to the roar of the delirious crowd.

———

"THUNDERSTORM AND PEPSI MEYERS SEND YANKEES TO THE POST-SEASON" shouted the New York Times the next day. "GOD SENDS RAIN, PEPSI SAVES SEASON" trumpeted the Daily News. The New York Post blared

"PEPSI, WE LOVE YOU ALL OVER AGAIN," its front page showing a photo of the outfielder flat on his back with his hand and ball thrust heavenward. The Jewish daily *Hamodia* presented its own perspective—"FROM DANCING IN SHUL TO DANCING IN THE OUTFIELD," —while the *Baltimore Sun* lamented, "GOD AND MEYERS TEAM UP TO BURY O's." Coverage of the game was everywhere. Replays of the catch, the subsequent on-field pandemonium, and the clubhouse celebrations dominated the airwaves and sports sites. The image of Pepsi Meyers being carried on the shoulders of his teammates from center field to the dugout was precious. The kid's face and hair were covered with flecks of mud, and he was completely disheveled. His glove had been snatched away by fans gone wild, as had been his cap and yarmulke. His uniform shirt was torn in several places, and the fringes of his tzitzis had been ripped off at each corner. But somehow, despite all attempts to pry it from his fingers, Pepsi had held on to the ball. As his bumpy ride approached the infield, his face beaming with joy, he held up the ball for the fans, who roared their appreciation of the young hero. Later that night on eBay, everything was sold. Even the tzitzis went for thousands of dollars apiece. No one was quite sure how eleven sets of strings managed to be auctioned off, but eventually someone caught on and the bidding was shut down.

I'm not going to bore you with all the details, but the Yankees went on to sweep the division series against Cleveland and to prevail in six over Oakland in the American League championship series. The World Series against the Los Angeles Dodgers was particularly sweet. They won the opener 4-1 behind Matthew Slade at Chavez Ravine. He struck out fifteen Dodgers, avenging the historical game-one loss to Sandy Koufax, who had done the same to the Yankees in the Bronx back in 1963. Although they lost the second game, they won the next three in succession, bringing the New York Yankees their thirty first World Championship at home in the Bronx. Pepsi Meyers's scintillating play was not affected by the pressure of the post-season. Over the fourteen-game span, he batted .432, smacked three home runs, and managed to drive in fourteen runs. This was accomplished despite the fact that he missed the two Friday night and one Saturday afternoon games. Ironically, the Yankees won all three of those contests. At the conclusion of game five, Damarcus Pendelton handed the young superstar the trophy naming him MVP of the World Series. A few days later, it had company on the mantelpiece as, to no one's surprise; Pepsi

Meyers was named Rookie of the Year and MVP of the American League.

Over two million people lined Broadway for the ticker-tape parade through the Canyon of Heroes in Lower Manhattan. It was an unseasonably warm early November day, and the players and their delirious fans were mostly bedecked in shirtsleeves as New Yorkers celebrated the unexpected success of their beloved team. Fans shouted the names of various players as they passed by in open cars, with the loudest cheers reserved for the tandem of Pepsi Meyers and Matthew Slade. By the way, Matthew was the recipient of the Cy Young Award in the American League. This was the twentieth time in baseball history that the Cy Young and MVP awardees were on the same team. It was the first time that any of the teammates, let alone both, were rookies. All in all, it was a wonderful day. Pepsi and Matthew were given keys to the city of New York by its beaming mayor, who pronounced with hubris, "Every once in a while, we let the rest of the country enjoy the championship trophy. For the past little while, we've been a bit too generous. But now that it's back where it belongs, I guarantee that the title World Series Champions will be staying here in New York for years to come." His words were greeted spontaneously with a cadenced cheer that went on for several minutes, "Thirty-two, thirty-two, thirty-two!" Amid all the revelry, the news release that the Yankees would be holding a press conference the next morning at the stadium flew mostly under the radar.

"Hey, Mel," said the AP reporter as the Yankee GM walked into the presser.

"Are you going to announce a renewal of Drake's contract this morning?"

"Have patience, Jim," Rapp answered, as he sat down in the middle of three seats set up behind the table. There were also three microphones on the table.

"You'll find out in a minute what this is about."

Rapp was followed into the room by Mickey Drake and, to the surprise of the entire press corps, a yarmulke-clad Pepsi Meyers. Melvin Rapp began to speak. "Ladies and gentlemen, Pepsi Meyers is going to read a prepared statement. He will not take questions from you after his remarks. At that point in time, he will leave this press conference. Mickey and I will be glad to answer your questions afterwards."

Melvin had to tap on the microphone several times before the room settled down. Once it did, Pepsi started reading from a prepared statement. "Ladies and gentlemen of the press, and to all Yankees fans everywhere, I am announcing today that I am taking an indefinite leave of absence from the game of baseball."

There was an explosion of noise as reporters hurled questions at Pepsi from all across the room. "Settle down, everybody!" Rapp shouted, tapping on the mike. "You're all professionals, aren't you? Follow the protocol we established, please."

The clamor slowly subsided, and Pepsi continued, "As you all know, that together with my parents, I have recently become somewhat acquainted with the rich tradition and complex set of laws and values that Torah Judaism is comprised of. I remain woefully ignorant of its most basic tenets, not having had the opportunity earlier in life to know of or study it. I truly wish that I could put off this quest until after my playing days are over, but I hope that Yankees fans can understand that to do so would be a betrayal of my responsibility as a Jew, which is to learn about and live by the heritage of my forefathers. The reason I have decided not to take any questions is because I know that for many of you out there, including many members of the Jewish faith, no answers I can give will fully satisfy you. All I can do is hope and pray that no fan or member of the Yankees family considers my decision to be a betrayal. I am only doing what I hope you all can agree is every man's task, to be true to his or her conscience in matters of faith and of the heart."

Pepsi paused for a moment to take a sip from the bottle of water on the table in front of him. "I have asked my agent, Jason Stern, to engage a lawyer on my behalf to review my contracts with the Yankees, Major League Baseball, network and online broadcasters, and any and all corporations with whom I signed to promote their wares. I agree to enter arbitration with all of the above if my obligations to them will not properly be met as a result of my upcoming leave of absence. I have further requested the services of Rabbi Sender Friedenson of Lakewood, New Jersey. He is a Talmudic scholar and this country's leading expert in Jewish contractual law. I want to be assured that any financial obligations I may have as a result of Torah law will not be overlooked. "

Pepsi flipped to what seemed to be the last page of his statement. "This past year has been the most wonderful of my young life. Being part of the magnificent Yankees organization and playing with such amazing teammates and for such devoted fans is something I will never forget. Baseball is America's pastime, America's signature sport. It epitomizes competitiveness, strategy, skill, and grace. I will certainly miss it."

Pepsi's voice cracked as he voiced this last sentence. He paused for a moment to wipe away a tear before continuing. "Perhaps there will come a day when I will feel secure enough in my Judaism to be able to return to the game. Of course, I would do so only if I were granted the dispensation to put Torah law first, as I was so graciously allowed to do these past few months as a member of the New York Yankees. And nothing would please me more if I do return than to play again in pinstripes. But if this past season will prove to be my only year in professional baseball, it will be because my soul has been drawn to a higher calling. I truly hope that everyone out there listening today can appreciate and respect my need to answer that call, and will bear me no malice for doing so. God bless you all. Thank you and goodbye."

And that was it. Pepsi Meyers stood up, turned, and walked out of the hushed room without looking back. Only once he exited did the momentarily stunned group of veteran reporters regain their bearings and start firing away at Melvin Rapp and Mickey Drake. "When did you find out about Pepsi's decision to quit baseball?"

"The Yankees knew about it before the start of the World Series," Mickey said. "We all agreed not to publicize it until after it was over."

"Did you try to talk him out of it, Mel?" asked Google Sports.

"No. I tried doing that once before and learned my lesson. The kid knows what he wants to do, and I think we all ought to respect his decision."

"Where's Pepsi going to study, Mel?" asked a reporter from Newsday. "Yeshiva University?"

"I've been told that he, his parents, and his grandmother will all be moving to Israel. If I'm not mistaken, they plan to live in Jerusalem. I do not know where he intends to study."

Thankfully for the tandem at the table, the *New York Post* reporter turned the subject back to baseball. "Mickey, who's gonna play center field for the Yankees next year?"

"I'm not sure, John," answered Drake. "But I'm sure we'll be able to find someone to upgrade the position." His response was met with a mixture of laughter and groans. "But kidding aside, our scouting department has identified some promising outfielders and although we're drafting last, we think some of them will be available when our turn comes up."

"We've also not ruled out looking at the available free agent market or making a trade or two," Melvin Rapp added. "Look, even without Pepsi Meyers, we will be the defending world champions. We remain a very good team, and with the reigning

Cy Young award winner to anchor our pitching staff, I would caution everyone not to take the New York Yankees for granted next year."

A few more perfunctory questions were asked, but only one story mattered, and everyone was eager to file it. Pepsi Meyers, the most promising talent in the history of baseball, was walking away from the game.

———•—•———

When Rabbi Elias emerged from his late morning Talmud class, he noticed that Sam Harris of the New York Times was waiting for him outside the Torah Center. Harris wrote for the Lifestyle & Religion section of the paper, and had done a comprehensive piece on the Riverdale Torah Center a few months prior, after Pepsi announced that he would no longer play on Shabbat.

"Rabbi Elias, have you got a few minutes for a quick interview?" Harris asked.

Rabbi Elias glanced at his watch.

"I'm meeting with someone in a few minutes Sam, but if you walk me home, I can give you as much time as that will take," Rabbi Elias replied.

"Thank you, Rabbi. I appreciate it," The reporter said.

They started walking up Independence Avenue.

"I'm curious, Rabbi. In the few months since I interviewed you, what impact has Pepsi Meyers' decision to become observant had upon your Center?"

"As you can imagine, it created an enormous spike of interest in Judaism, not only in Riverdale and the greater New York area. Pepsi's story has impacted Jewish communities across the nation and overseas. Israelis in particular have been affected by the fact that an American superstar has chosen to embrace Torah. I'm told that many of the outreach programs over there are being swamped."

"But don't you think that Pepsi's announcement this morning will be harmful to your cause?"

"Why would I think that?"

"C'mon, Rabbi. How many people can afford to walk away from their jobs in order to go off and discover their faith? The Meyers hit the jackpot with the draft and are more than financially secure. But I would think it would scare away anyone else of lesser means, or anyone who enjoys their profession for that matter, who's thinking of joining your program and becoming observant."

"Do you think I advised Pepsi to leave baseball to go study Torah?"

"Didn't you?"

"No, I did not. I'm delighted with his choice, of course, and like you said, he has the means to do so. But Pepsi and his parents made that decision completely on their own. Look, Torah observance rarely, if ever, will necessitate that a person give up his career. There was a time over a century ago when one could not find work if he observed the Sabbath. It was an incredible test of faith for Jews of that era to remain Torah observant. But today, virtually any legitimate vocation will be compatible with Torah. Of course, along the way, the person should be doing his very best to continue growing and discovering his heritage. But to ask for more is not mandated by the Torah and in fact, would be counterproductive to it."

The Rabbi stopped walking and turned to the reporter as he arrived in front of his house. "I want to thank you, Sam, for your question. I didn't realize that people might react that way. So I hope that what I just told you will make it into the paper."

"It won't just make the paper, Rabbi. Pepsi's story will be on the front page."

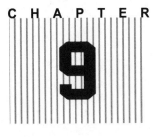

CHAPTER

9

I Knew I Was Gonna Take The Wrong Train... So I Left Early.

Lawrence Peter (Yogi) Berra

It had been a hectic few weeks for the Meyers since the end of the World Series. They had made a quick trip to Israel and their impression of the country only increased their confidence that they were making the right choice. Their first stop was a moving encounter at the Western Wall in Jerusalem. The depth of emotion they all felt being where the Holy Temple once stood caught them by surprise. It seemed that their nascent journey back into the embrace of Judaism had already connected them profoundly to the storied ground they were standing on. Many American tourists, and some black-hatted Yeshiva students from New York, recognized Pepsi. Tactfully, they refrained from disturbing what they must have known was his first encounter with the Wall. Afterwards, Joe and Emily began their search for the right community in which to live as well as the best geriatric care facility for Grams. Pepsi was tasked with identifying which Yeshiva program would be most attractive to him. Several days later, mission accomplished, they returned to New York with the intention of returning to Israel in time for Chanukah.

In between several trips to Binghamton, and with the help of the Eliases and others in the community, the family was packed and ready to go. Joseph, Emily, and Pepsi were invited by Rachel to come over for dinner the night before their morning flight from JFK. To their surprise, many of the Torah Center's congregation and staff had discreetly made their way over earlier in the evening and were there to turn what the Meyers thought was going to be a quiet dinner into a rousing send-off party. There was music, drinking, dancing, and of course several speeches, not to mention tearful hugs and sincere assurances to stay in touch.

"Please promise that you all will come and visit us whenever you're in Israel," Emily implored her friends. "We've rented a large apartment, and there are two guest rooms that we'd love to know will be kept occupied."

Rabbi Elias clanged a spoon on a glass to get everyone's attention. "Quiet everyone, please. I'd just like to say a few short words. No long speeches, I promise!"

When the room settled down, he commenced. "It has been an incredible summer. Our community has had the good fortune to host and meet this most wonderful family. As much as we'd love for them to stay with us, we recognize and applaud their decision to move to Jerusalem. May we all merit doing so as well."

Rabbi Elias paused as several people murmured "amein" to his words. He continued.

"Next week is the holiday of Chanukah, when we light the menorah. Here in Riverdale and throughout the Diaspora, where Jews are but guests in a foreign land, it is kindled in the privacy of one's home, indoors. But in Jerusalem, the custom is to light it outside. We know you're finished packing, and probably don't have extra space for a toothpick, but somehow you have to find room for this."

The rabbi bent down and retrieved a gift bag, which he put on the table. He held up its contents for all to see. "This antique brass menorah has a glass enclosure. Even on a windy night, the flame is protected and the olive oil will burn sufficiently for you to fulfill the requirement. An inscription has been engraved on the back of the menorah, and I'd like to read it."

A memento for our dear friends Joseph, Emily, and Pepsi Meyers. Your brief but meaningful sojourn in our community has touched us all. We wish you great success and fulfillment in the Holy Land.

"מקום שבעלי תשובה עומדין צדיקים גמורים אינם עומדין"

"Even the perfectly righteous cannot stand
where returnees to Torah stand."
The Torah Center of Riverdale, New York

Somehow details of the Meyers' schedule leaked, and there were hundreds of well-wishers at the airport the next morning to see them off. Jews, many from the nearby Five Towns community, as well as fans from all over the city, turned up to catch one last glimpse of their hero. Not surprisingly, the media was also present. Pepsi was pushing Grams in a wheelchair, while Joe and Emily walked beside a porter who had their many suitcases piled high on a dolly. As they approached the executive check-in counter, shouts of "Good Luck Pepsi," "We Love You Pepsi," and "B'hatzlacha" could be heard from all across the hall. Yeshiva students started singing Shlomo Carlebach's "Yerushalayim," and spontaneous dancing ensued. Though they tried, the boys were unable to get Pepsi to join the circle. The festive atmosphere continued while the Meyers were being interviewed by security but waned as they approached the gate leading to the scanning checkpoint. From that point on, they would be out of sight to the fans. Realizing this, Pepsi turned and waved to the throng, eliciting one last loud and final cheer.

The cameras caught it all. A young eight-year-old blond haired boy wearing a number eighteen Pepsi Meyers pinstriped jersey managed to get Pepsi's attention, and asked the last question just before he entered the gate heading for security.

"Pepsi, can you please tell us when you'll be coming home?"

Pepsi turned towards the boy, thought for a moment, and replied, "I am going home, kid. That's exactly where I'm going."

The End

———•••———

TORAH
CONNECTIONS

I f *The Season of Pepsi Meyers* has sparked an interest in discovering more about Torah & Judaism, the author recommends the following online resources, listed in alphabetical order:

Afikimfoundation.org - Offers an array of educational websites for all ages, including an interactive site with web conferencing technology.

Aish.com - Since its launch in February 2000, Aish.com has become the leading Jewish content website, logging over a million monthly user sessions with 380,000 unique email subscribers.

Aishdas.org - The AishDas Society empowers Jews to utilize their observance in a process for building thoughtful and passionate relationships with their Creator, other people and themselves.

Arachimusa.org - Outreach, education, and support of Jewish men, women, and children towards living a life of Jewish values, Torah, and mitzvos, the strengthening of the Jewish identity, and assimilation prevention across the globe.

Chabad.org - Chabad-Lubavitch is a philosophy, a movement, and an organization that promotes Judaism and provides daily Torah lectures and Jewish insights. Chabad Houses across the globe serve as Jewish community centers; offering Torah classes, synagogue services, and assistance with Jewish education and practice.

Jewishexperience.org - The Manhattan Jewish Experience is a cutting edge program for young Jewish professionals in their 20's and 30's, with little or no background in Judaism interested in connecting more to each other, to Judaism and to the community at large.

Naaleh.com - Naaleh Torah Online offers thousands of audio and video Torah classes from some of the best Torah teachers.

Ncsy.org - NCSY is the premier organization dedicated to connect, inspire and empower Jewish teens and encourage passionate Judaism through Torah and Tradition.

Njop.org - NJOP reaches out to unaffiliated Jews, offering positive, joyous Jewish experiences and meaningful educational opportunities.

Ohr.edu - For more than 30 years, Ohr Somayach has been instilling Jewish pride in university students the hard way – through knowledge.

Oorah.org - Oorah's mission is to reach out to Jewish families everywhere with life-enhancing learning opportunities, resources and programs – all with a warm, human touch.

Ou.org - The Orthodox Union provides an array of religious, youth, social action, educational, public policy and community development services, programs and activities.

Partnersintorah.org - Offers Jewish adults of all backgrounds across North America a cost-free learning opportunity to discover Judaism – its culture, history, and traditions – at their pace and their schedule.

Shabbat.com - For those interested in experiencing the joy and tranquility of Shabbat for the first time, this resource will make a connection with families across the country, that are eager to host them.

Torah.org - Offers Jewish educational material, Torah archives and online learning opportunities.

Torahanytime.com - Records and uploads to its website, Torah lectures given across the globe.

The world is invited to come and watch them, free of charge.

Torahmedia.com - Thousands of free mp3 audio downloads and a lending library of thousands of world-class Jewish speakers and scholars.

Webyeshiva.org - Video-conferencing technology that offers real-time, round the clock, interactive classes…taught by outstanding Rabbis and teachers.

———◆———

Readers are encouraged to visit the website:
Pepsimeyers.com

The author welcomes comments and questions regarding *The Season of Pepsi Meyers* and can be reached by writing to:
info@pepsimeyers.com

GLOSSARY of TERMS

The words in the Glossary are Hebrew, unless otherwise specified.

Abba	Father.
Aliyah	(lit.) To go up. (colloq.) To move to Israel.
Amein	Amen.
Amidah	The standing prayer.
Ashkenazi	Jew of European descent
B'hatzlacha	Be successful!
Chai	Life
Challah	A loaf of bread – usually braided – used for Shabbat.
Chanukah	The festival of lights.
Chilul Shabbat	Violation of the laws of Shabbat.
Chutzpa	Gumption.
Glatt	(Yiddish - lit.) Smooth. (colloq.) Kosher without question.
Halacha	Jewish law.
Hatzalah	(lit.) Saving (of lives). (colloq.) A community based volunteer emergency medical response team.
Havdalah	A prayer recited at the end of Shabbat.
Kaddish	The mourner's prayer.
Kippah	Head covering or Yarmulke.
L'chaim	To life!

Mamzer	(lit.) The child of an illicit relationship. (colloq.) An obnoxious person.
Menorah	A candelabra.
Mezuzah	A parchment with Torah verses affixed to the doorpost
Mussaf	An additional prayer recited on Shabbat and Holidays
Rosh Hashana	The Jewish New Year
Seder	A festive meal celebrated on the first night of Passover in Israel, and the first two nights of Passover in the Diaspora
Shabbat	The Sabbath.
Shana Tova	A good year.
Shiva	(lit.) Seven. (colloq.) The period of mourning for a deceased relative.
Shmini Atzeret	Jewish holiday immediately following Sukkot.
Shul	(Yid.) Synagogue.
Siddur	Prayer book
Simchat Torah	Jewish holiday celebrating the conclusion of the yearly Torah cycle.
Sukkot	(lit) Booths or huts. (colloq.) Seven day Jewish festival in Israel, eight days in the Diaspora.
Talmud	Extensive body of work (a.d. 400-500) that interprets the Torah and forms the basis of Jewish law and tradition.

Torah	The five books of Moses.
Tzitzis	Fringes attached to a four cornered garment.
Yarmulke	(Yid.) A Kippah or head covering.
Yerushalayim	Jerusalem.
Yeshiva	A school or academy where Torah is studied.
Yom Kippur	The Day of Atonement.
Zaydie	(Yid.) Grandfather.

About the Author

Abie Rotenberg needs no introduction to anyone familiar with the world of Jewish music. An accomplished composer and lyricist, he has proven to be a keen observer of human nature, with the ability to translate profound ideas into the written word. In particular, his many ballads on a variety of themes are renowned for subtly illuminating the radiance and beauty of the Jewish faith.

In his debut novel, Abie combines his passion for Torah and love of baseball by introducing a compelling character. Pepsi Meyers' struggle with the conflicting allure of superstardom and the call of timeless traditions newly discovered, is a groundbreaking amalgam of entertainment and inspiration.

Born in New York City, Abie Rotenberg is the father of six children and currently resides with his wife in Toronto, Canada.